MW01050998

FRONTIER ASSAULT

FRONTIER ASSAULT

The North Staffordshire Regiment in the
Third Afghan War, 1919

James Green

ISBN: 9781096217107

Copyright © 2019 James Green

The Author has asserted his right under the Copyright, Designs and Patents Act, 1988, to be identified as the Author of this Work.

All rights reserved. No part of this publication may be reproduced, stored in or introduced into a retrieval system, or transmitted, in any form, or by any means (electronic, mechanical, photocopying, recording or otherwise) without the prior permission of the author. Any person who does any unauthorised act in relation to this publication may be liable to criminal prosecution and civil claims for damages.

A catalogue record for this book is available from the British Library.

Maps: Michael Rutherford Graphic and Web Designer

Cover design: Michael Rutherford Graphic and Web Designer

To Staffordshire's infantry, past and present.

CONTENTS

Author's note

The North-West Frontier Province in the narrative which follows is today known as Khyber Pakhtunkhwa, an administrative province of Pakistan. Prior to the Partition of India in 1947, which created Pakistan, it was part of British India. As this text describes events that occurred between 1914–19, I therefore refer to the wider geographic area as British India, or just India, rather than Pakistan.

Although the correct nomenclature for the war is the *Third Anglo-Afghan War*, I have used the shorter form, the *Third Afghan War*, in the interests of simplicity. I have applied a similar approach for the names of military units. So, I abbreviate the 2nd Battalion The Prince of Wales's (North Staffordshire) Regiment as the 2nd North Staffords.

Where I have used place names, I have generally used versions that are in present-day use.

When you're wounded and left on Afghanistan's plains,
An' the women come out to cut up what remains,
Jest roll to your rifle and blow out your brains,
An' go to your Gawd like a soldier.

Rudyard Kipling, *The Young British Soldier*

Introduction

In 2001, a month after the September 11 attacks on New York City and Washington, D.C., the United States of America launched a war in Afghanistan. Code-named Operation Enduring Freedom, it aimed to deny the terrorist group Al-Qaeda a safe base of operations by removing the Taliban from power. America's closest military ally, the United Kingdom, backed the war and dispatched troops to join the fight. In so doing, the British returned to Afghanistan, for a fourth time.

There had been three previous wars between Britain and the Afghans. In the First Anglo-Afghan War (1839–42) and the Second Anglo-Afghan War (1878–81), the British invaded and occupied the country. Operation Enduring Freedom, at least to Taliban eyes, was similarly a war of aggression. Like these two earlier British wars, this most recent entanglement was not a short one. Combat operations lasted for thirteen years until 2014, and some foreign troops remained behind in training and support roles. Another similarity was that the aggressors lost. The Russians suffered a similar fate during the Soviet-Afghan War (1979–89). Great Britain, the Soviet Union, and the more recent US-led international coalition all ended up leaving Afghanistan; because they were worn down by insurgency or rebellion, suffered a military defeat, or else felt drawn to negotiate a face-saving exit deal.

The exception to these confrontations is the Third Anglo-Afghan War. Unlike the other wars, this was one of Afghan aggression and was entirely reactive on the part of the British. Although the British Indian Army crossed into Afghanistan, it did so only after a series of Afghan incursions into British India. There was no attempt at nationwide occupation, and the furthest British advance across the Afghan border was just thirteen miles. It was also a much shorter affair. The war barely lasted three months, from May to August 1919, and most of the fighting took place in the first four weeks. And, at least militarily, the British won.

Given these dynamics, one might be forgiven dismissing the war as one of the low-level agitations that the British faced in India's ever-restless North-West Frontier. Many in the British government and public did just that. It was poorly reported, with fewer than a dozen articles appearing in *The Times* of London, most buried in the middle pages. Instead, the country focused on domestic reconstruction following the devastation of the First World War. In the century that has passed since, historians have likewise given the Third Afghan War scant attention, treating it as a postscript to the world war.

But the Third Afghan War was not a minor deployment. It involved the mobilisation of 350,000 British and Indian troops, more than those in the First and Second Anglo-Afghan Wars combined. Operations spread across a front of 800 miles. In today's prices, it cost a third of a billion pounds sterling. There was widespread use of the modern weaponry that had emerged during the First World War, including the recently formed Royal Air Force (RAF). More significantly, the war had the real potential to spark unrest throughout the entire North-West Frontier. It could have ignited a call against colonial rule across India and threatened the existence of the British Raj.

There are a myriad of approaches to writing about wars. In the narrative ahead, I explain the war's strategic context and operational level events. But, to explore the battles, incidents and the men who fought the war at a more granular level, I have chosen to tell the story from the perspective of a single infantry unit - the 2nd Battalion The Prince of Wales's (North Staffordshire) Regiment.

The 2nd North Staffords was formed in 1881, in the same year that the Second Afghan War ended and in which it had a peripheral role. From 1903, following the Kitchener Reforms of the British Indian Army, it was stationed in India on garrison duties. A well-trained frontier unit, the 2nd North Staffords was one of only eight regular British Army battalions kept to defend the subcontinent during the world war. They were part of the initial force sent to halt the Afghan invasion. On their way to the war zone, they quelled an insurgency which could have undermined the entire British response. The battalion then played a crucial role in defeating the Afghan vanguard in a tenacious mountain assault in the Khyber Pass. Soon after, they were the first to cross the border into Afghanistan; the first British forces to enter the country since 1881. After the war, the 2nd North Staffords was the most decorated British unit of the entire force. Over eighty years on, their descendants, the Mercian Regiment, were one of the premier British infantry regiments that returned to Afghanistan during Operation Enduring Freedom.

CHAPTER ONE

A Restless Frontier (1914-1918)

The origins of the Third Afghan War lay in the secret war, fought in the Nineteenth Century, between the two most powerful nations on earth - Victorian Britain and Tsarist Russia. Those engaged in this shadowy struggle called it the *Great Game*, a phrase immortalised in Rudyard Kipling's *Kim*. At the heart of the game, was control of Afghanistan. For the British, Afghanistan was an essential buffer from Russian territorial ambitions for the defence of India - the jewel in the crown of the British Empire.

By the turn of the century, the *Great Game* had played out. With the signing of the Treaty of Gandamak at the conclusion of the Second Afghan War, Afghanistan ceded responsibility for their foreign affairs to the British. Thereafter, imperial intriguing tailed-off. In return for British guarantees of protection from Russian aggression, the treaty provided for the Amir of Afghanistan to be paid an annual stipend. For his part, the Amir undertook not to host foreign ministers or emissaries in Kabul, and to conduct his external affairs through Britain.

With the onset of the First World War, foreign powers renewed their interest in Afghanistan. Imperial Germany recognised that civil unrest, external attack, or other such actions in the Indo-Afghan region could weaken the British. This could limit the British Indian Army's availability to reinforce the fighting in Europe, the Middle East and elsewhere. Turkey also devoted more attention to Afghanistan, viewing the Muslim nation as one that might be convinced to aid its fight against the British and her allies.

German wartime activity towards Afghanistan began as early as August 1914 when it assembled the initial elements of a diplomatic mission. The mission, which soon became a Turco-German initiative, arrived in Kabul in August 1915. Its purpose was to convince the Amir of Afghanistan, Habibullah Khan, to side with the Central Powers and declare war on the British. Internal factions pressured Habibullah to turn against the British, to show solidarity with their Muslim brethren fighting the *jihad* declared by the Turkish Sultan. Cautious of the British reaction, Habibullah played for time. He denied the diplomats an audience until October 1915 and was noncommittal in the negotiations that followed. By spring 1916, the Germans realised that Habibullah was unwilling to join them and the mission left Afghanistan, leaving a small party in Herat until October 1917. But, while foreign influence in Afghanistan generated no serious concerns for the British during the First World War, the tribes that lived either side of the frontier were less acquiescent.

India's border with Afghanistan, the Durand Line, stretched for 800 miles. It led from an off-shoot of the Hindu Kush mountains in the north. From there it meandered southwards through the hills of the Waziristan and Suleiman ranges, down to the semi-desert ranges north of the Makran coast near Quetta. As the formal border cut through difficult to reach mountainous areas, the British established an administrative border, ranging in parts out to 280 miles east of the Indo-Afghan frontier. British and Indian troops guarded and policed this inner border at the edge of the foothills, leaving the space in between alone.

This mountainous zone was home to two million Pathans and other Pashtun tribes, who considered themselves aligned to their Muslim brethren in Afghanistan. It was estimated that the tribal territory could muster 200,000 anti-British fighters, many armed with rifles, although muzzle-loaders were still common. They were experienced hill fighters and were formidable adversaries, ruthless, courageous and cunning. A contemporary war correspondent described them to be *'natural robber tribes, living in mountain passes and preying as opportunity offers on their weaker neighbours. Independent, hating control, warriors by birth, by training, and by instinct, fighting is their normal life'*.

The most troublesome region was the North-West Frontier Province, which formed the northern part of the Indo-Afghan border. It was centred on the Khyber Pass, one of the few mountain passes between Afghanistan and India capable of being transited by a military force. The area was a constant source of agitation and conflict. By the early 1900s, Anglo-Indian units had been engaged on the frontier for over a hundred years. They guarded the administrative border, maintaining a loose level of security using British-officered, locally recruited tribal militias, and mounting punitive expeditions when the tribesmen became too restless.

So, while India mobilised almost a million men for service overseas during the First World War, Army Headquarters decided to keep behind the regular British Army units of the three frontier divisions. Alongside Indian units, which were hollowed out, just eight British infantry battalions and two cavalry regiments were left on the subcontinent. The British authorities gambled that this 'thin red line' would be enough to defend India from attack, but it was not long before this assumption was tested.

The first tangible threat to British authority on the frontier materialised in November 1914 after the Turkish Empire's entry into the First World War on 29 October. It took place in Waziristan – a troublesome Pashtun-dominated district in the North-West Frontier Province's southern section. Stirred up by *mullahs* and the Sultan of Turkey's call for a *jihad*, 2,000 tribesmen from Afghanistan's Khost Province crossed the border and gathered in the Tochi Valley. The *lashkar* was swiftly defeated by the North Waziristan Militia, but not before Army Headquarters had dispatched reinforcements. These included the 2nd North Staffords, who were temporarily transferred from the 2nd (Rawalpindi) Division to the Bannu Brigade at short notice. At that time, Major Edward Fox commanded the battalion which had a strength of twenty-five officers and 800 other ranks. It comprised a headquarters, four rifle companies and a machine-gun section, supported by a quartermaster, transport, signals and medical elements.

There was a further advance by the Khostwal tribesmen in early January 1915, but the militia successfully halted this without the need for reinforcements. Captain Eustace Jotham, 51st Sikhs (Frontier Force), was awarded the Victoria Cross during this action. A former North Staffords' officer, Jotham had transferred across to the Indian Army in 1905. He was commanding a dozen of the militia when they were surrounded by a force of 1,500 tribesmen. He gave the order to retire, and could have himself escaped, but sacrificed his own life attempting to rescue one of his men who had lost his horse. This was the first of two Victoria Crosses awarded for actions in India during the First World War.

In March 1915, the North Staffords returned to their peacetime garrison at Rawalpindi. Although they saw no substantive action during this deployment, the battalion received two casualties. Private J. Ferries and Private J. Holeyhead died from sickness or disease.

Gradually, news of the call for a *jihad* and the thinning out of Anglo-Indian forces to fight on the Western Front spread. As it did, other tribesmen on the frontier agitated against British authority. After the Tochi Valley attack there were six other *lashkars* in the first half of 1915. They varied in size, with the largest a gathering of 15–20,000 tribesmen who attacked a fort and outposts in the Swat Valley. In all cases the enemy were routed, but the general sense created was one of a frontier under siege.

In late August, emboldened by the Swat Valley uprising, large groups of Mohmand tribesmen gathered on the administrative border, just north of the key northern city of Peshawar. They had raided from the border towards the British fort at Shabkadr in January 1915 and had come back in April with a larger force of 2,400 tribesmen. Both attacks were unsuccessful, but the Mohmands were committed to testing the resolve of the Anglo-Indian troops. Shabkadr had been the focus of many Mohmand attacks, most notably in the 1890s. In response to this third *lashkar*, Army Headquarters ordered a mounted column and two brigades to Shabkadr and a mobile column to Abazai. These were sub-ordinated to the 1st (Peshawar) Division, commanded by Major General F. Campbell.

On 29 August, the 4th Infantry Brigade, led by Brigadier G. Christian, received orders to respond to the imminent threat from the Mohmands. The 2nd North Staffords were one of four infantry battalions in this brigade. The others were the 35th Sikh Regiment and the 30th and 84th Punjab regiments; each of which were Indian units, in line with the normal composition of British Indian brigades. The battalion organised themselves and left their summer camp at Gharial in the Murree Hills the next day. They started the campaign with a trying forty-five-mile road march, much of it under a hot sun, to the railhead at Rawalpindi. From there, they moved west, by rail, to Peshawar, where they halted for twenty-four hours. After sunset on 2 September, the battalion marched north-east to Adozai, a British fort on the administrative border, crossing several tributaries of the Kabul River by barge bridges on route. They arrived at midnight and set up bivouacs. At dawn, the men marched on to Shabkadr Fort, further north. On arrival, they rested and prepared a perimeter camp.

The hurried deployment was warranted as, on 3 September, locals reported large groups of tribesmen moving in the foothills and preparing sangars near Hafiz Kor. This was a small village which abutted the administrative border four miles north-west of Shabkadr Fort. For the North Staffords, first sight of the hostile Mohmand tribesmen came on 4 September. Elements of the battalion were part of a brigade probing operation a mile north of Shabkadr when hostile Mohmands appeared on the formation's left flank. The brigade's cavalry scouts met the threat with a few skirmishes until the tribesmen withdrew. By mid-afternoon the encounter was over, and the battalion returned to their makeshift camp at Shabkadr.

By the evening of 4 September, the hostile force had reached 10,000 men, four times larger than the Mohmands had assembled in their last cross-border incursion in April. They were spilling out of the foothills and into the relative open plains around Hafiz Kor. Concerned that the Mohmands' numbers would grow, Major General Campbell ordered the 1st Division, now 8,000 men strong, to attack the tribal force the next day. The divisional plan was to attack on a broad front; with the 2nd North Staffords tasked to create a firing line on a ridge to the west of Khwaja Banda village, a

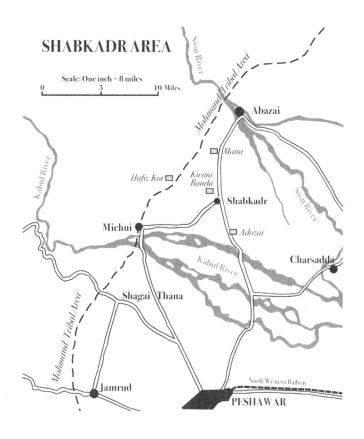

mile north of Shabkadr. They would then hold down the enemy as other troops attacked the *lashkar's* flanks.

At 6.30 a.m., the battalion advanced in two lines. A and C companies were in the forward firing line, led by Officer Commanding (OC) C Company, Major Henry Tweedie, a veteran of the Second Boer War. B and D companies, with the commanding officer, and the battalion's Vickers machine gun, followed. They secured the ridge without incident and from there observed handfuls of tribesmen retiring west towards Hafiz Kor. A mile further towards Khwaja Banda they got to within rifle range of the village. They went static there while the machine gun was hauled up to the front. Those Mohmands who remained in the village were set on defending their sangar positions. A firefight ensued, supported by shelling of depth positions by the brigade's mountain artillery battery. It soon became evident that the battalion had superior strength and more of the tribesmen withdrew in the face of heavy rifle- and machine-gun fire. By 9 a.m. just small parties of snipers remained, but they proved to be able marksmen and the battalion suffered several casualties. After a lengthy engagement the Vickers – capable of firing accurately out to over a mile – together with individual marksmen in the leading companies, silenced a handful of the snipers.

The enemy who had superior numbers if not firepower, *'resisted stoutly and displayed great bravery, tenaciously holding on to their sangars'*. But they *'were defeated with heavy loss and driven from their positions'*. At around 1 p.m., after a four-hour battle, the brigade headquarters ordered the forward firing line to retire. It fell back through the supporting companies and afterwards through the 84th Punjabs, the brigade's reserve. The staged retirement back to Shabkadr was controlled by OC A Company, Major J. W. Ley. It took an hour and a half but the enemy did not pursue, and the fight was broken-off.

Elsewhere on the battlefield, the Mohmand tribesmen had tried an advance on Shabkadr Fort, manoeuvring to the south of the North Staffords' position. As they approached, the field guns of the artillery opened on them, but the tribesmen kept on, threatening the left flank of the Anglo-Indian forces. Major General Campbell deployed a mounted column to halt the advance. Squadrons from the 21st Lancers, 14th Lancers and a mounted battery of the Royal Horse Artillery conducted a cavalry charge. It proved the decisive action of the divisional attack, but it was not without losses. Of the five 21st Lancers' officers who took part in the charge, the tribal fighters killed four, including the commanding officer, Lieutenant Colonel Scriven. Private Charles Hull was awarded the Victoria Cross for his role in saving the life of the Adjutant, the only officer to survive.

In their first day of battle, the 2nd North Staffords had taken the fight to the enemy and blunted the tribesmen's resolve. They had acquitted themselves well. But, not all survived. Private G. H. Johnson was killed in action and, later that day, Private D. Toft died of his wounds. Seven others were injured, including the Adjutant, Captain Alfred Punchard.

The next day, 6 September, the battalion was involved in a follow-up operation against the Mohmands at Hafiz Kor. This time, the North Staffords had rotated to be the brigade's reserve. The brigade conducted an artillery bombardment of the village, but no infantry engagement took place and the 4th Brigade fell back to Shabkadr. Shortly after sunset, shots were fired at the North Staffords' perimeter camp. A clearance patrol led by OC B Company, Captain A. S. Weldon, searched the crop fields to the north of the camp and returned having killed a few tribesmen. In the morning the battalion left Shabkadr and retired to Adozai, several miles to the south. Here they set up another perimeter camp with 4th Brigade. The battalion remained at Adozai for several weeks and was inactive during that time.

At the end of September, the *mullahs* stirred up the Mohmands again. In early October, several *lashkars*, numbering 9,000 men, returned to Hafiz Kor. After receiving fresh orders, the battalion moved back up to Shabkadr with haste. The first week of October was spent setting up defences. No enemy action was reported, apart from two night-time sniping shots against the camp. One of these wounded a corporal from the battalion.

Major General Campbell decided to take the offensive again and to attack the Mohmand tribesmen on 8 October. The 4th Brigade was given a forward role and the 2nd North Staffords' A Company, led by Major J. W. Ley, was tasked to be the advance-guard. A Company led the battalion and brigade north from Shabkadr and then west towards Khwaja Banda village. The 30th Punjabs formed the brigade's left, while the North Staffords were on the right, with the 84th Punjabs in reserve. The initial advance was uninterrupted. Then, a mile from the village, the battalion encountered a few Mohmand snipers. It was likely these were acting as sentries, for shortly after advancing further, the battalion became engaged in an intense firefight with a larger force. Still some distance from the enemy, the brigade's No. 8 (Mountain) Battery from the Royal Garrison Artillery (RGA) began an artillery bombardment.

The 10-pounder field guns, effective out to just over two miles, were brought to bear to suppress the Mohmands. These enabled the battalion to shake out and set up a firing line with A and D companies forward. They were supported by several Vickers machine guns from the 114th Mahrattas in the centre. During this engagement, a North Staffords' officer, Lieutenant B. D. Cox, and four other ranks were wounded.

One of these men, Private Henry Chadwick, died the next day. After the initial firefight, the firing died down on both sides as the tribesmen gradually abandoned their positions. Other divisional forces pursued the enemy on the flanks. In the mid-afternoon the division ordered the brigade to retire back to Shabkadr. It did this through successive firing lines, each providing cover for the move rearwards.

The dispositions of the Mohmands and the 1st Division's attack plan were like that of the engagement on 5 September, a month earlier. Again, despite initial strong opposition, the tribesmen were defeated and withdrew to the foothills. This occasion was noteworthy because armoured cars were used for the first time in actual fighting in India. They proved of great value both in reconnaissance work and in covering the movements of the cavalry.

After the skirmish on 8 October, the rest of the campaign passed without incident for the 2nd North Staffords. The battalion moved east back to Rawalpindi – their peacetime base – staging at Adozai, Taru Jabba and Nowshera for several weeks each as the threat from tribal activity reduced. At Taru Jabba, east of Peshawar, the battalion was held in a cholera isolation camp for a week. No fresh cases of cholera developed during their enforced stay, although one soldier died from cholera contracted earlier, and two soldiers died from dysentery. On 9 December, the battalion entrained at Nowshera and arrived back at Rawalpindi the same day.

On the battalion's inspection report for 1915–16, Major General Campbell wrote:

This fine Battalion came temporarily under my command in the field during operations on the North-West Frontier last year. It proved a very valuable unit. Right through the Regiment I observed determination, elan and good cheer. It manoeuvred remarkably well and smartly and, as regards fighting efficiency, I have nothing but praise to record of it. It showed up well in all circumstances.

General Sir Beauchamp Duff, Commander-in-Chief, India, further praised the North Staffords and other British and Indian troops. He recorded that they *'showed a fine spirit and great cheerfulness and were eager and ready at all times to march and fight'*. And, that the operations *'were so successfully carried out in spite of climatic conditions which must have demanded the greatest endurance on the part of the troops'*. Later, the regiment was awarded the battle honour 'North-West Frontier, 1915' for its role in the 1915 campaign.

During 1916 and into 1917, the tribes on the North-West Frontier continued to cause trouble sporadically, but not at the scale of 1915. There were further operations for the British Indian Army. These included another Mohmand attack at Hafiz Kor in November 1916, dealt with by the militia forces and troops stationed closer to the administrative border. None of these operations required the support of the 2nd North Staffords; apart from a short week-long mobilisation in early October 1916. In late August 1917, the North Staffords transferred to the 45th (Jalandhur) Brigade in the newly formed 16th Indian Division. After three months in Jalandhur, in November 1917, the North Staffords moved camp to join the 1st Division's 2nd (Nowshera) Brigade. They remained in Nowshera for the rest of the world war, going on to fight with the 2nd Brigade in the Third Afghan War.

Compared to the fighting and losses suffered on the Western Front, the actions on the Indo-Afghan frontier during the world war were slight. Still, one should not underestimate events on the North-West Frontier. The prompt actions by the Anglo-Indian forces and the severe reverses inflicted on the tribal invaders demonstrated British resolve and preserved the frontier in comparative peace. Alongside the foreign threats to security in India, the securing of the frontier enabled the British to continue to send troops to other theatres. More significantly, the British Raj had been maintained.

So, by the end of the world war, the Indo-Afghan border region had not presented the British with any sizeable challenge. There had been no mass uprising of the frontier tribes. And, while Habibullah had entertained the advances of Germany and Turkey – hedging against a British defeat – he abided by the country's treaty obligations and maintained Afghanistan's neutrality. By doing this, he was of immense help to the British. At the same time, foreign interest in Afghanistan and growing anti-British sentiment convinced Habibullah that he needed to assert Afghanistan to be an independent nation. He came around to believing that independence was a just reward for his nation remaining neutral during the war. On this basis, in January 1919, he demanded a seat at the Paris Peace Conference, which followed 11 November 1918 armistice. Frederic Thesiger, 1st Viscount Chelmsford, the Viceroy of India, swiftly refused the request. This angered the anti-British establishment in Kabul and started a series of events that led, four months later, to the Third Afghan War.

CHAPTER TWO

'Stand to!' (19 February-8 May 1919)

Just as an assassination was the catalyst for the First World War, another sparked the Third Afghan War. On the night of 19/20 February 1919, Amir Habibullah Khan was shot dead by a colonel in the Afghan Army. The true reason for the attack is not known, but it was probably motivated by the Amir's continued alliance with the British in the face of increasing Afghan nationalism.

Habibullah's third son Amanullah declared himself Amir, but so did Nasrullah, Habibullah's brother. After a brief political struggle, Amanullah prevailed and imprisoned Nasrullah for the murder. Suspected of having plotted his father's death, Amanullah spent the first few months of his reign bolstering his authority. He focused on exploiting anti-British nationalist sentiment. To divert attention from internal strife, he sensed advantage in pursuing a goal to free from Afghanistan from British control. He viewed this, as his father considered before him, a just reward for Afghanistan's allegiance to the British during the war. Again, the request was cold-shouldered by Viscount Chelmsford in Calcutta. This rebuke was unacceptable to the new Amir, who needed to oppose British influence to hold on to power.

Amanullah's next step was unexpected and audacious. He decided to invade British India. An invasion was more than sabre-rattling, but his rationale for taking this action was unclear. He may have believed he could push the British into granting independence; or even aspired to retake the North-West Frontier Province. After all, the province had originally been part of Afghanistan until it was lost to Sikh expansionism in 1820–34. Even more ambitious, Amanullah may have hoped that an attack on India's border would spark a revolution that ended British control of India. In the limited press coverage of the war, other reasons were put forward. *The Times* speculated that:

Some of the causes of the Afghan troubles are still obscure, but there is reason to suspect that Russian intrigue has had something to do with them. A friendly Russia which recognises her duty to the rest of the world would have no motive to stir up trouble of this kind. But a Russia with its hand against everyone, like the present Bolshevik Government of Russia, can create endless mischief.

Whatever his objectives, limited or otherwise, Amanullah's course of action was not as reckless as it might first appear, for several plausible reasons. First, despite Allied success, the First World War had shown those in the colonies that British imperial power was not the unbeatable military might they had assumed it to be. Across the British Empire there were minor attempts at altering the balance of power in the post-war era. Afghanistan, it must be remembered, had been victorious against the British in the First and Second Anglo-Afghan Wars. Perhaps now was an opportunity for further success?

Second, the Amir knew that the defeat and humiliation of Turkey during the First World War intensely aggrieved the Muslim border tribes. They had been stirred up by Turkey's entry into the war in October 1914 and showed their anti-British sentiment throughout 1914–18. Multiple *lashkars* formed sporadically on the periphery of the administrative border. Well-armed and formidable fighters, they had an acute wish for revenge against the British.

Third, the Amir may have believed that the Indian Government was too distracted by internal matters to concern itself with events on the frontier. Shortages of food, goods and transport had led to massive increases in prices, compounded by a forty per cent taxation increase to finance the war. These and other wartime pressures created significant discontent amongst the population and a growing call for Home Rule. By early 1919, the Government was faced with low-scale civil unrest throughout India. This culminated in rioting throughout the principal towns of western India in March and April, including the infamous Amritsar massacre on 13 April.

Finally, Amanullah gambled that the Anglo-Indian troops would be too war weary to resist. When the Afghans attacked, it happened at a difficult time for the British.

With the end of the First World War only a few months earlier, troops were exhausted and disenchanted. Those in India, mostly reserves and territorials [sent there to relieve regulars for fighting elsewhere], *were anxious for demobilisation, while the line regiments were all due for home service. The Indian Army, which had sent overseas more than a million men, was also tired* [and desiring their long-awaited post-war leave].

Amanullah sought to exploit these factors. His strategic plan was to show strength and intent by amassing several Afghan Army brigades at multiple points on the Indo-Afghan border on a wide front. This, it was hoped, together with a formal declaration of war and initial military successes in the loosely controlled tribal areas, would ignite a general uprising amongst the frontier tribesmen. If this was achieved, the Afghan regulars could be bolstered by 100-200,000 tribal fighters. British militia forces would likely then desert, at which point the balance of the Afghan Army could commit to the invasion. While the tribal force caused havoc and dissipated British forces in response, the Afghans would then be in a favourable position to attack key military objectives. Amanullah gambled that the agitating anti-British elements in India would seize this moment to revolt. This would not only interfere with the British military response to the Afghan invasion but provide for acquiescent border towns. The Afghan forces could link up with and seize these with relative ease. A general insurrection could force the British and Indian governments to grant the Afghan demands so it could concentrate on domestic affairs. Successfully executed, the plot might hasten the fall of the British Raj.

It was an ambitious plan, particularly given the state of the Afghan military. At the beginning of hostilities in 1919, the regular Afghan Army comprised a 50,000-man standing army. It consisted of twenty-one regiments of cavalry, seventy-eight battalions of infantry and 280 breech-loading guns; albeit just under half of these units were stationed on the frontier with India. Smaller than the British Indian Army, the Afghans were ill-equipped and lacked the manoeuvrability and professionalism of their opponents. A British officer who served in the war gave this evaluation of them:

Afghan regular units… were ill-trained, ill paid, and probably under strength. The cavalry was little better than indifferent infantry mounted on equally indifferent ponies. Rifles varied between modern German Turkish and British types, to obsolete Martinis and Snyders. Few infantry units had bayonets. Artillery was pony drawn, or pack, and included modern 10cm Krupp howitzers, 75mm Krupp mountain guns and ancient 7 pounder weapons. There were a few, very old, four-barrel Gardiner machine guns. Ammunition was in short supply and distribution must have been very difficult. For the artillery much black powder was used, both as a propellent and bursting charge for shells. The Kabul arsenal workshops were elementary and mainly staffed by Sikh artificers with much ingenuity but little real skill. There was no organised transport and arrangements for supply were rudimentary.

Based on this assessment, the Afghan regular army was incapable of taking on the British by itself. It depended upon the active support of the tribes on both sides of the border. If the Amir was to stand any chance of success, he needed the tribes to bolster his attack force and disrupt the British lines of communication.

To prepare the ground, Amanullah undertook three measures in early spring 1919. First, he summoned the heads of the trans-border tribes, explained his proposal and urged them to back it. Their support was vital:

The tribal offensive was the basis of the whole plan; and the line of action of the Afghan Army depended entirely on the extent to which tribes consented to cooperate and on the later success of their operations. Their best and only chance of success lay in securing the cooperation of the tribes and in coordinating their efforts.

He then dispatched money to tribal leaders and issued arms and ammunition at Jalalabad and elsewhere to assure their support. Next, the Amir contacted Afghan agents and revolutionary groups in India. He sent funds to these groups and counselled that they ready themselves for action. Lastly, Amanullah sent his Commander-in-Chief, Saleh Muhammed Khan, to the Afghan border settlement of Lowyah Dakka at the western end of the Khyber Pass. He was accompanied by an escort of two infantry companies and two guns. Amanullah informed the British about this but explained the reason as a precaution to maintain security, should any civil disturbances in India spread to Afghanistan. When all was ready, Amanullah proclaimed a *jihad* against Great Britain.

After Amanullah's proclamation on 3 May 1919, he ordered more of his army to move to the Indo-Afghan border. Another 2,000 troops were sent towards Dakka to support Saleh Muhammed in the Khyber. A further 2,000 men were sent to Khost in the central border region and 1,500 were dispatched to Kandahar in the south. On the same day, a party of Afghan tribesmen under the leadership of Zar Shah, a notorious Shinwari raider, carried out the first hostile acts of the war. His men first turned back a detachment of Khyber Rifles escorting a convoy through the Khyber Pass near to Landi Kotal Fort. This was the small British border garrison which guarded the western end of the Pass. By doing this, Shah effectively closed the border. Later, his men killed five unarmed road labourers at the water works which fed the garrison at Landi Kotal. Both actions occurred on the British side of the border. Intelligence reports on the proclamation, the movement of Afghan troops and the border incidents in Landi Kotal were received by the British by late afternoon. Tentatively, with the Afghan intent not fully understood, Headquarters North-West Frontier Force tasked a small column of infantry to prepare to reinforce Landi Kotal.

Early on 4 May, the Afghan regulars moved up into the Khyber from Dakka. They crossed into British-Indian territory at Torkham and pushed a mile west into the Pass, halting at Landi Khana. Here the deep gorges and hairpin bends of the Khyber road opened into a valley where there was a small border dwelling surrounded by a range of grey, barren hills. The fort at Landi Kotal lay three miles further

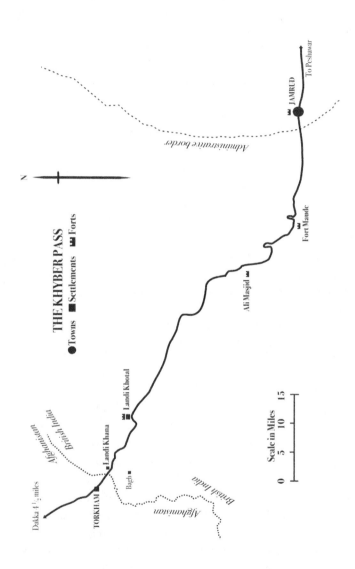

THE KHYBER PASS
● Towns ■ Settlements ▦ Forts

N

To Peshawar

JAMRUD

Administrative border

Fort Maude

Ali Masjid

Landi Khotal

Afghanistan
British India

Landi Khana

TORKHAM

Bagh

Afghanistan
British India

Dakka 4½ miles

Scale in Miles

0   5   10   15

east. Saleh Muhammed set up defensive positions on two of these hills, the Khargali Ridge and the Kafir Kot Ridge. Together these dominated the western exit from the Khyber Pass into Afghanistan. He then sent 350 troops and two guns to occupy the Spin Tsuka and Tor Tsappar ridges, five miles due north of Landi Kotal.

The garrison was manned by a sizeable force of 500 men from the locally recruited Khyber Rifles. But, the quantity and quality of these troops would likely be insufficient to withstand a concerted attack. Next, the Afghans took control of an upland pasture known as Bagh and its nearby springs. Close-by they also seized the springs at the head of the Tangi *nullah*, a gorge which led up into the hillside west of Landi Kotal. Together, the springs provided much of the water for the garrison. Additionally, the Afghans captured a pumping station, which lay midway between the springs and the fort. Signalling their intent for war, the Afghans then cut the water supply.

As the springs and waterworks provided the main water source for Landi Kotal, their capture by the Afghans was significant. The garrison had a reserve tank and small supplies from other springs, but neither could adequately sustain the fort area. Given that it was nearing the height of the summer, an adequate water supply for men and animals was vital. Without one, the British would have struggled to concentrate a large enough force at Landi Kotal to eject the Afghans. So, the Bagh and Tangi springs became strategically important and recapturing them imperative.

Later in the day, down in Peshawar, the Afghan Postmaster in the city, Ghulam Haidar, started distributing large numbers of leaflets he had collected from Jalalabad. These contained a *firman* signed by the Amir. It announced, falsely, that the Germans were backing the Afghan invasion, and that Egyptians had risen against British rule. Amanullah wrote that he believed that the people of India had been ill-rewarded for their loyalty during the First World War and were justified in rising against the British. Then the Amir stated that his army would move down from the Khyber, with support from the tribes, and free the Indian Muslims. He called on all Muslims to join the *jihad*. More practically, he encouraged them to revolt against the Indian government. And, to *'use every possible means to kill British, continue to tear up railways and cut down the telegraph'*.

On 5 May, news of the Afghan occupation of the Bagh Springs reached Peshawar. This triggered the dispatch to Landi Kotal of the reinforcements which had been placed on standby two days earlier. These comprised a company each from the 1st Infantry Brigade's 1/15th Sikhs and the 1/9th Gurkha Rifles. A section of engineers and miners, and two 3.7-inch howitzers of No. 6 (Mountain) Battery RGA were in support. They moved in 30-cwt lorries and reached Landi Kotal the same day. In parallel, more Afghan regulars moved into the positions at Bagh and the Khargali Ridge. Concurrently, elements of the force at Tor Tsappar and Spin Tsuka advanced south to within a mile of Landi Kotal. Once there, they seized the Ash Khel Ridge to the north-east of the fort. Fortunately, the Afghans didn't exploit the opportunity to seize the small garrison at Landi Kotal before the British reinforcements arrived. By late evening on 6 May, the Afghans had assembled two infantry brigades (eight battalions with cavalry) and one pack artillery brigade on the Khyber front. Three of these battalions and two guns lay on the British side of the border. The other five battalions, cavalry and six guns at Dakka, were thirteen miles back from Landi Kotal in Afghan territory.

By now, British intelligence reports gave a relatively accurate picture of Afghan intentions. The Amir was planning to launch a simultaneous attack into British territory at three points along the border with India. These were to travel via the Khyber to Peshawar, from Khost into Waziristan and from Kandahar into Balochistan. It was expected that the main Afghan thrust would be through the Khyber Pass. The attacks would take place within ten days. They were to be accompanied by coordinated actions to mobilise the support of the frontier tribesmen, together with orchestrated riots in India designed to tie up British troops.

Keen to forestall an extended entanglement with the Afghans, Viscount Chelmsford telegraphed London. He informed the British Government that *'I have ordered overwhelming force up in order that an excuse may be found for peaceful retirement* [of the Afghans]'. Chelmsford then issued a formal declaration of war. This led to Army Headquarters in Calcutta suspending all the many demobilisations, disbandments and reductions that were ongoing after the First World War; together with immediate mobilisation of the 1st (Peshawar) Division, the 2nd (Rawalpindi) Division and other frontier units.

Realising that the reinforced garrison at Landi Kotal would be over-matched by the amassing Afghan force, the British dispatched the balance of the 1st Brigade to the Khyber. On 7 May, the brigade's British infantry battalion, the 2nd Somerset Light Infantry with two sections (four guns) of No. 8 (Mountain) Battery RGA, were moved up from Peshawar. They were smuggled passed the Khyber tribesmen in covered lorries. The brigade's other infantry battalions, the 1/35th Sikhs and the rest of the 1/9th Gurkhas and 1/15th Sikhs, followed on foot. Two troops from the 30th Lancers, No. 77 Battery from the Royal Field Artillery (RFA) and a machine gun company accompanied them. By 8 May the whole brigade had arrived, with the lead elements of the 2nd Infantry Brigade close behind. This, it was hoped, would be enough to relieve Landi Kotal, neutralise the Afghan advance-guard and to eject the Afghans from British territory.

With the mobilisation of troops ordered, Army Headquarters organised British forces into two commands. North-West Frontier Force, commanded by General Sir Arthur Barrett, was responsible for the Khyber. Operations in the central and southern border areas were managed by Lieutenant General Richard Wapshare's Balochistan Force. Together these forces comprised ten cavalry regiments, fifty-five infantry battalions, twenty-three batteries of artillery, seven armoured car companies, ten machine gun companies, engineers and signallers. To support these fighting troops was an ancillary tail of medical units, logistics units and others, that was equivalent to two or three times the numbers of fighting men. The total deployed force far exceeded the pre-war strength of the Indian Army.

In the North-West Frontier Force were the 1st and 10th Cavalry brigades, the 1st Division and the 2nd Division. These were supported by one brigade in the Kohat-Kurram area, two brigades in Waziristan, Corps troops and the Frontier Militia. Internal security troops for Peshawar added to the force. The closest division to the Khyber Pass was 1st Division, based in Peshawar, which was also home to Headquarters North-West Frontier Force. It was now commanded by Major General C. A. Fowler. His divisional troops included the 4th and 38th batteries RFA, No. 6 and No. 8 (Mountain) Battery from the RGA, plus 77th (Howitzer) Battery RFA. Alongside these were sappers, miners, and Nos. 263 and 265 Machine Gun companies equipped with sixteen Vickers guns carried on lorries, animals or armoured cars.

Within the 1st Division, the 1st Infantry Brigade, based in Peshawar, was the first to be called to action. It is from this brigade that the initial reinforcements for Landi Kotal had been dispatched. 1st Brigade also sent the 2nd Somersets and other units which followed on 7 and 8 May. Next in line were the 2nd Infantry Brigade units. They lived in the military cantonment at Nowshera, twenty-seven miles due east of Peshawar on the line of the North-West Railway. Commanded by Major General S. H. Climo, the 2nd Brigade's major units included the 2nd North Staffords, who had transferred to the brigade in November 1917. Like other infantry brigades, the 2nd Brigade followed the convention of the time of having one British battalion and three Indian battalions. Alongside the North Staffords were the 1/11th and 2/11th Gurkha Rifles, and the 2/123rd Outram's Rifles. The 3rd Infantry Brigade was headquartered at Abbottabad, further east.

Compared to the seasoned battalion that fought the North-West Frontier campaign in 1915, the 2nd North Staffords was a different unit. Although it had been ordered to stay in India during the world war, many of the experienced regular army officers and men had left India to fight overseas. These included, in August 1916, a draft of thirty-two other ranks to reinforce the 7th North Staffords. A similar draft was sent to the 8th Welsh Pioneers, both for service in Mesopotamia. Individual officers who served outside India included Major Tweedie, OC C Company. He served with the South Staffordshire Regiment and was wounded-in-action in France. Captain Punchard, the battalion's adjutant - who had been wounded in the battle of Hafiz Kor - also volunteered for overseas service. He was killed-in-action in Basra, Mesopotamia in March 1917. Others fought in those theatres and in Gallipoli and Persia. By 1919, the 2nd North Staffords' strength had reduced by a third, to twenty officers and 538 other ranks. Of those who remained, around sixty per cent were either volunteers or conscripts who had joined the regular battalion since 1915. Only five officers in the battalion fought in both the North-West Frontier campaign and the Third Afghan War. The others, and a good proportion of the men, had never fired a rifle in anger. Incidentally, in the intervening years the commanding officer, Major Fox, was promoted to Lieutenant Colonel. His new adjutant was called Captain E. A. Squirrell, the forest animal themed names causing the men much amusement.

After they had been stood-to on 5 May, the 2nd Brigade started to move to the Khyber. Receiving deployment orders at 2 p.m. on 7 May, the North Staffords was the last of the four battalions to leave Nowshera. A rushed afternoon and evening followed as they readied themselves for war. Once the battalion's equipment was packed, they moved to the railhead and boarded trains for the short journey to Peshawar. They arrived in Peshawar at 5 a.m. the next morning and set up a bivouac site on the race course. Brigade headquarters ordered them to stage there until called forward to move up to Landi Kotal. While they waited, the 1/11th Gurkhas headed for Landi Kotal, with the 2/123rd Outram's following.

In the meantime, as the Afghans swarmed into the Khyber, the British faced a further challenge. On 7 May, the Criminal Investigation Department received intelligence that Ghulam Haidar, based in Peshawar, was working alongside the India Revolutionary Committee to organise a revolt in the city. The revolt, scheduled for the next day, planned to amass 8,000 men. Arms had been smuggled into the city and Haidar's plan was for the mob to burn the military cantonment and government buildings, along with the railway and storage buildings. This, it was hoped, would severely disrupt the British response to the Afghan invasion and be the start of a general insurrection. *'The gravity of the situation will never be realised for the inflammatory speeches and lies spread, broadcast by "politicians" amongst the ignorant classes had occasioned such a state of mind that it needed but a spark to set the whole Frontier ablaze'* recorded Randolph Bezzant Holmes, the North-West

Frontier Force's official photographer. So, while defending the garrison at Landi Kotal was pressing, the more immediate threat was now to secure Peshawar.

An important provincial capital and military cantonment, Peshawar was just thirty-five miles from the Indo-Afghan border. It is the first city reached when travelling down from the Khyber Pass. As was common amongst Indian and Afghan towns and cities, Peshawar was surrounded by a high wall built from brick and mud. The total perimeter was five miles along which, at irregular intervals, there were sixteen gates. Holmes gives us this description of Peshawar:

The City commanded by Fort Bala Hissar extends to the east and has much of interest in it. It is encircled by walls and buildings, the main inlets having gates that are sentried and closed at night. The chief gate is named after Edwardes, a distinguished Commissioner, and the main thoroughfare passes through this into the Khissa Khani bazaar, or place of stories, where rumours are retailed. Who does not remember the city when once seen with its narrow tortuous streets and alleyways running between uneven plastered buildings that tower at dangerous angles, being held together by wooden framework, and looking anything but safe; the host of whitewashed mosques with their domes, minarets, and spires rising in every conceivable direction; and then the thoroughfares and bazaars thronged with jostling, noisy, virile humanity.

The insurgent threat had been anticipated, in part, as there had been a steady growth in agitation in Peshawar since the start of the year. Increasingly large public meetings aimed at promoting Hindu-Muslim unity against the British were being held, yet no violence or direct action had been taken. Events in Amritsar in April (later known as the Jallianwala Bagh massacre) were fresh in people's minds. In anticipation of likely trouble, the annual rotation of troops to the hills for

James Green

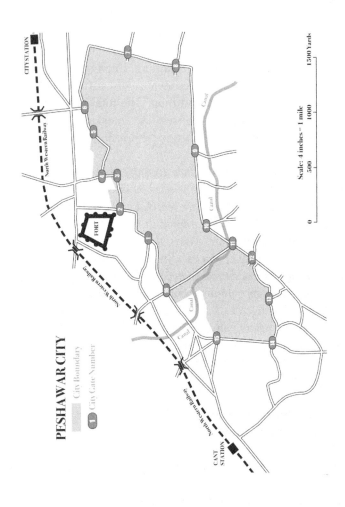

31

the summer was suspended, military staffs were placed on 'Stand to' and plans had been drawn up for a cordon of troops to be placed around the city in the event of an emergency.

The maintenance of law and order in Peshawar was vital, due its role as a command location and staging point for troops moving up to the Khyber. Insurgent control of the city would have done much to booster the Amir's call to arms. For that reason, upon arriving in Peshawar, the 2nd Brigade headquarters, the 2nd North Staffords and the 2/11th Gurkhas were disembarked there, rather than continuing onto the Khyber Pass. Reinforced by the 1st King's Dragoon Guards and two companies of armoured cars, the brigade was tasked to secure Peshawar City.

Orders were given in the mid-morning and the operation began at 2 p.m., when it was expected most of the Afghans would be resting after their midday meal. With the armoured cars leading, the brigade left off from the railway in four columns, the cavalry circling the outer walls of the city at speed. As they did so, they dropped off detachments to hold each gate. Pursuing on foot, the North Staffords and the Gurkhas then took over the defence of each gate, deploying a platoon at each. Once the infantry was in place, the 1st King's Dragoon Guards reconstituted to become the brigade reserve. Within eleven minutes, the cavalry had closed all the gates and within forty-five minutes the infantry cordon was in place, with all exits from the city sealed off.

Thereafter followed a period of stand-off as the British political officer demanded, by proclamation, for the population to give up the agitators. If they did not, the city's water supply would be cut. Unsurprisingly this had the desired effect. By 11.30 p.m., Ghulam Haidar and twenty-two revolutionaries had surrendered. Nine others had left the city before the cordon operation. With the uprising over, the city settled down for the night. An hour after sunrise on 9 May, the 2nd Division's 6th Infantry Brigade arrived to takeover Peshawar's security. After being relieved by the Royal Sussex Regiment, the 2nd North Staffords' platoons then marched back to the battalion's bivouac at the race course.

It is possible that the planned insurrection would not have taken hold and spread wider. But, many of the city's garrison troops had deployed up to the border and others were not in Peshawar at the time of the crisis. The vacuum this created bolstered support for the insurgents. A successful revolt could have prompted the Afghan regular force, supported by frontier tribesmen, to advance down from Landi Kotal and seize Peshawar. Had the North Staffords and other troops not contained the threat, the British defence of Khyber would have been severely compromised. In the first twenty-four hours of their deployment, the battalion had secured a notable success, without even firing a shot. Martial law was imposed in the city and wider province. The focus of the battalion – and the rest of the 2nd Brigade – now switched to getting up into the Khyber, as swiftly as possible.

CHAPTER THREE

Assault on the Frontier (9 May-14 May 1919)

While the 2nd Brigade dealt with the Peshawar situation, events up in the Khyber Pass were moving on at pace. At Landi Kotal, the British garrison was under threat from the west and the north, with the closest enemy grouping just a mile away. Loss of the garrison would have been a huge propaganda coup for the Afghans. The 20,000 Afridi, Mohmand and Orakzau tribesmen of the Khyber hills observed events carefully. An Afghan military victory stood set to give the Amir a flag of success to rally the frontier tribes. To prevent this, the British made plans for a counter-attack on 9 May.

Despite having five battalions and a battery of artillery forward, the Afghans opted not to attack on either 6 or 7 May. Instead, they strengthened their hold on the Bagh Springs, awaiting further forces to move up from Jalalabad and not expecting the British to have reacted with such speed. This delay was critical. It allowed time for the 2nd Somersets to arrive in Landi Kotal on 7 May. They were followed the next day by the rest of the 1st Brigade and the 1/11th Gurkhas from the 2nd Brigade.

To defend Landi Kotal and expel the Afghans, Brigadier G.

F. Crocker, commanding the 1st Brigade, now had a force of equivalent size to the Afghan regulars. To prepare for an attack, he first deployed the 1/35th Sikhs, 1/9th Gurkhas, 30th Lancers and some Khyber Rifles. These were assigned to cover positions on the ridges north and north-west of Landi Kotal. Their purpose was to protect the garrison from a flanking Afghan attack. This was fortuitous, as when occupying the Ash Khel Ridge, the troops discovered a party of Afghans trying to seize the ridge. A small encounter followed, which resulted in the Afghans withdrawing back to their main positions at Tor Tsappar and Spin Tsuka.

As a preliminary operation, Crocker tasked a company-sized group from the 1/9th Gurkhas and one from the 2nd Somersets to occupy two prominent hills. Suffolk Hill, a mile south-west of Landi Kotal, lay on a line towards the Afghan position. Securing it was key to preventing an Afghan advance on the fort area. Range Hill was two miles to the south-east of Suffolk Hill. The Afghans had not sought to occupy either of these and the 1st Brigade troops captured them without incident.

Crocker was left with three infantry battalions for his main attack; the 1/15th Sikhs, 1/11th Gurkhas and the rest of the 2nd Somersets, supported by the artillery. His infantry reserve was the 2nd Brigade's 2/123rd Outram's, who had made a risky night march through the Khyber on 8/9 May to support the attack.

The brigade plan was for the Somersets to reinforce Suffolk Hill to cover the advance. Then, the 1/15th Sikhs were to capture an Afghan outpost established on Bright's Hill. This was a small feature half a mile ahead of Suffolk Hill and just 800 metres from the Bagh Springs. From there, the Sikhs and 1/11th Gurkhas would advance westwards. They would retake the Tangi Springs and waterworks and then oust the Afghans from their positions in and behind Bagh.

As dawn broke on 9 May, the attack launched. A company from the Sikh battalion captured the Bright's Hill outpost before the daytime Afghan outpost troops had arrived. From there, the remaining troops pushed on to other outposts around Bagh. However, they soon found themselves outmatched by an Afghan force supported by covering positions on the Khargali and Kafir Kot ridges. British batteries, firing from positions near Landi Kotal, lacked the range to have any real impact on the ridges, and by 8 a.m. the infantry attack had stalled. Sensing failure, Crocker gave the order to halt the attack and the two assaulting battalions came to a standstill 700 metres short of the Bagh Springs. To protect their gains, the troops spent the rest of 9 May digging in defences.

In the opening salvo of the Third Afghan War, the Afghans had defeated the British force. Crocker had allocated too few of his battalions to the assault and his fourteen field guns and mountain guns had been ill-sited. Modern-day estimates suggest that it requires a force ratio of 5:1 to attack an enemy in defence. Even had Crocker attacked with all five battalions, this would have given him a 2:1 ratio and may too have proved inadequate. It was an ominous start for the British. But, the attack had recovered the Tangi Springs and the waterworks, enabling a much-needed water supply to Landi Kotal to be restored. The Afghans now had the opportunity to reinforce their advance-guard and move to occupy Landi Kotal. This would have denied the British any workable space in the Pass to concentrate a force of enough size to launch a counter-attack. If this happened, removing the Afghans from the Khyber would have been extremely difficult. Whichever side could muster enough troops to attack first would hold the Pass for the foreseeable future. British hopes now lay on the 2nd Brigade getting to Landi Kotal before the Afghans could bring more troops up from

Dakka.

As the British attack began in the Khyber, the 2nd Brigade headquarters, 2nd North Staffords and 2/11th Gurkhas were restarting their move west from Peshawar. The brigade struck camp and returned to the railhead where they boarded trains for the twelve-mile journey to Jamrud Fort; the eastern entrance to the Khyber Pass. Here, the railway ended and the Peshawar Plain gave way to the Spin Ghar (or Safēd Kōh) mountains, part of the Hindu Kush range.

After halting for a few hours at Jamrud to transfer equipment onto camels and mules, the brigade then marched west up into the Pass. The route was by a gravelled road; the only one of its kind in the region. It was a tortuous march. Laden with their weapons and fighting gear, the men had to ascend 300 metres in height, over eleven miles, battered by dust storms and scorching breezes. Their initial destination was Ali Masjid. This was the first staging point for camel caravans and others who normally transited the Pass. It had been the scene of many skirmishes and disasters in the two earlier Anglo-Afghan wars.

Assigned as the brigade's advance-guard, the 2nd North Staffords (less B Company) led the march. The 2/11th Gurkhas followed, along with the remaining sections of No. 6 (Mountain) Battery RGA and No. 285 Machine Gun Company. The 2/123rd Outram's, 1/11th Gurkhas and the other artillery and machine gun sections had gone ahead while the brigade had conducted the Peshawar operation. B Company were the brigade's rear-guard, escorting an animal train carrying equipment for the Outram's.

As they endured the forced march, the sight of two single-seater Sopwith Camel biplanes flying low over them, broke the tedium felt by the troops. Crewed by the RAF, the biplanes were heading to drop bombs on the Afghan forces at Dakka. This was notable, as it was the first use of offensive aircraft anywhere in the whole of South Asia.

Although the route to Ali Masjid was purportedly secured by piquets from the Khyber Rifles, this was not to be true. For as B Company followed up the rest of the brigade, a group of Afridi tribesmen fired on them. Six soldiers, including Company Sergeant-Major Hallam, were severely wounded in the ambush. Chaos ensued as the panoply of animals in the convoy scattered in all directions. OC B Company, Captain Frank Hatton and Second Lieutenant Edward Horseman, commanding Nos. 5 and 6 platoons, gripped the situation. Horseman counter-attacked with his men, while Hatton organised the company and convoy. Their robust response killed three of the tribesmen, wounded eight, and forced the others to flee back into the mountains. The North Staffords had fired their first shots of the war.

Unluckily for the Afridis, Hatton and Horsemen were no strangers to the *'crack and thump'* of enemy fire. Hatton, age 27, arrived in India in November 1914. He was one of the handful of battalion officers that served in both the North-West Frontier campaign in 1915 and this return to the frontier. Horseman joined the army in 1914, as a private in the Royal Warwickshire Regiment. He served in France in 1915 and 1916 until he was invalided home with severe shell shock and a wounded right thigh. I mention this detail, because later in the narrative he gets wounded again, in the left leg; poor chap. After recovering from his first injury, Horseman returned to France in early 1917. He commissioned as an officer into the Worcestershire Regiment (29th/36th of Foot) in March of that year. Horseman stayed in the army after the world war and transferred to the 2nd North Staffords in February 1919.

Dealing with the attack's aftermath delayed the brigade for an hour, as casualties were evacuated to Peshawar and animals gathered. Unhindered for the rest of the march, the

2nd Brigade was complete in Ali Masjid by 8 p.m.. Bivouacs were set up and the troops rested for the night.

Ali Masjid was a flat expanse surrounded by hillside, on the far side of which was a deep gorge bordered by towering cliffs. This lengthy, narrow defile presented the archetypical image of the Khyber Pass. Dominating the entrance, on an isolated spur, stood Ali Masjid Fort. That evening, the fort was occupied by two companies of the Khyber Rifles. By the next morning, 10 May, 2nd Brigade found it empty. Locally recruited levies, the Rifles had felt the pressure of their tribes to support the Afghan invasion and had abandoned their post.

There was concern that the defile presented an opportunity for further ambushes by the tribesmen or deserters from the Khyber Rifles. In view of this, Major General Climo spent the first few hours of the day putting in place his own troops to secure the gorge entrance and piquet the route. Once these were in position, the brigade marched through the gorge and on to the next staging point at Landi Kotal, where the Pass opened out onto another large valley. The nine-mile march passed without incident and Landi Kotal Fort was reached by late afternoon. Encircled by low ranges, the valley was protected by block house piquets manned by troops from the 1st Brigade. Here, the 2nd Brigade consolidated itself and got ready for the mission ahead.

Major General Fowler, General Officer Commanding (GOC) 1st Division, had reached Landi Kotal late on the 9 May, a day earlier. He took over command of the operation from Brigadier Crocker. With the 1st Brigade fixed in position, but wanting to keep the initiative, Fowler planned a second attack on the Afghan positions.

As the 2nd Brigade arrived in Landi Kotal, the divisional headquarters briefed them on the enemy dispositions and issued orders. At 5.30 p.m., Major General Climo took the 2nd

Brigade's commanding officers to the summit of Suffolk Hill. From there they got a glimpse of the enemy positions before sunset. Still held by the 2nd Somersets, Suffolk Hill was a mile-and-a-half south-east of the forward enemy positions. From this hill the recce party could observe the Afghan force on the Khargali Ridge and around Bagh. Although it had sustained casualties from the earlier attack, the Afghans still had five battalions, and one pack artillery brigade deployed on the British side of the border. This grouping was part of a larger divisional-sized force reported to be building-up on the Dakka Plain, under ten miles away. Below the Afghan positions, were those occupied by the 1/15th Sikhs and the 1/11th Gurkhas, whose attack had failed.

To eject the enemy advance-guard, the British now had available eight infantry battalions. To support them were an assortment of artillery from No. 77 Battery RFA, No. 8 (Mountain) Battery RGA, and No. 6 Battery RGA. Plus, two machine gun companies, which had twenty-two Vickers guns. 1st Brigade troops were given fire support or flank protection tasks to help the 2nd Brigade attack. Bolstered with a machine-gun section, the main body of the 2nd Somersets was ordered to occupy Rocky Knoll. This was a spur 500 metres from the enemy's furthest right position on the Khargali Ridge. That right-hand position had been designated as the 2nd Brigade's break-in point and the North Staffords' initial objective. From Rocky Knoll the Somersets could bring fire onto it from an angle oblique to the assault. The 1/15th and 1/11th would give more fire support from their positions at the base of the Bagh Springs until the assaulting battalions passed through them; after which they would reconstitute as follow-on assault troops. The howitzer and gun batteries would initially fire on the forward enemy positions. They would switch to depth targets after the break-in had started and be prepared to neutralise any flanking

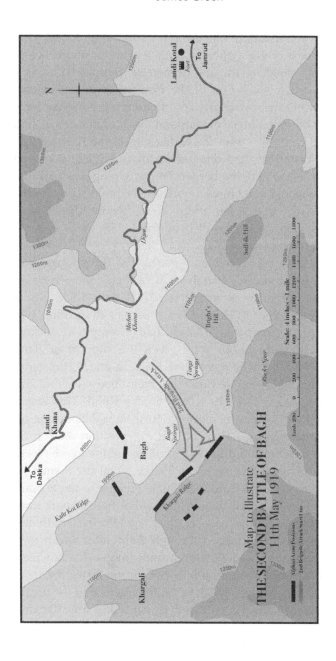

Map to Illustrate
THE SECOND BATTLE OF BAGH
11th May 1919

enemy counter-attacks. Fowler kept the 1/9th Gurkhas and 1/35th Sikhs back at Landi Kotal. The former in reserve and the latter covering the northern approach to the fort area from enemy attack. This left Major General Climo with three of his four infantry battalions; the 2nd North Staffords, 2/11th Gurkhas and 2/123rd Outram's. All three would be committed to the brigade's assault.

After the reconnaissance, the 2nd Brigade spent the night of 10/11 May preparing itself for the attack. Climo planned a 'one-up' assault, with the North Staffords leading. They were tasked with breaking-in to the right flank of the Afghan position on the Khargali Ridge. The 2/11th Gurkhas were to follow close behind, breaking off right midway through the assault to attack the enemy's centre. Once they did, the 2/123rd Outram's, the brigade's immediate reserve, had to be ready to either reinforce a stalling assault or to exploit success. At 4.30 a.m., dawn, the battalions left their positions around Landi Kotal's cemetery. They marched the two miles down through the hairpin bends and deep gorges of the Pass. They passed Suffolk Hill and halted at the base of Bright's Hill, half a mile further. Company and platoon commanders went up to the summit and the Afghan positions were pointed out to them. With the final recce complete, the battalions then moved up to the dead ground behind the 1/15th Sikhs, forming successive lines of two platoons abreast. Ahead of them, on higher ground, lay a coordinated defensive position of sangars and trenches, manned by an enemy emboldened by their successful repulse of the British attack two days earlier.

Given the narrowness of the terrain, Lieutenant Colonel Fox planned an echeloned formation for the North Staffords. B Company to lead, followed by D Company and C Company. After leaving the forming-up position, A Company would move off to the left flank to give rifle- and machine-gun fire support onto the forward enemy trenches. Luckily, since the earlier campaign in 1915, the battalion had been issued with the lighter Lewis Gun. This replaced the Vickers gun which needed six to eight-men to move and operate it.

In position at 7.48 a.m., the battalion lay and waited for H-Hour. Meanwhile, the Somersets manhandled the Vickers guns up to Rocky Knoll, as the carrying mules had found the ascent to the fire support position too steep. At 8.30 a.m., the British attack started with an artillery bombardment of two rounds a gun per minute. Two minutes later, the machine guns with the Somersets engaged the enemy position, having just got in place. At 8.38 a.m., B Company left the cover of the dead ground and crossed their notional line of departure.

On passing through the 1/15th Sikhs and 1/11th Gurkhas, the North Staffords came under fire straight away. Their right flank was hit by enemy at Bagh and on the Kafir Kot Ridge. Several soldiers were wounded. D Company diverted to suppress the fire from these positions, which they did so successfully, that when the 2/11th Gurkhas broke cover, they were able to start their advance without suffering casualties. B Company pushed on, but their advance was tortuously slow. It took over two-and-a-half hours for them to fight their way up 850 metres, through the rocky outcrops, to reach the forward enemy trenches. Not only was the *'ground very difficult and* [the] *final ascent very steep'*, the battalion had to endure the searing heat (over 50° centigrade in the shade). The heat and the steepness of the slope made it necessary for them to halt at intervals to re-form and to get their breath. During these periods of immobility, the British guns and machine guns would cease fire. After an interval they would re-open and the North Staffords would press on. B Company's commander, Captain Hatton, was later commended for the courage and commitment he displayed leading this most critical part of the attack. Despite the severe conditions, incoming rifle fire from both flanks and a stubborn Afghan defence, the company pressed on steadily. As the advance progressed, the British supporting batteries silenced the Afghan artillery; giving partial relief to the infantry.

Eventually, at 10.30 a.m., B Company reached the first trenches on the crest of the ridge. Just before they broke in, the men of the leading platoons were so close to the bursting shells of the British artillery, that they were stained yellow by lyddite fumes. Many of them vomited from inhaling the lethal smoke. As the men fixed bayonets to their rifles, the howitzers shifted their fire onto the enemy's centre. Second Lieutenant Horseman, who led the response to the Afghan ambush two days earlier, commanded the first platoon to reach the objective. He led the assault into the enemy's trenches, shooting down three of the Afghans with his Short Magazine Lee-Enfield Rifle. The rest of the company rushed forward to reinforce the break-in and clear the position. Some of the enemy fled to the south and south-west, where they were caught by the fire of the Somersets and of the four machine guns posted with them. Those who survived withdrew to a series of sangar positions which formed a second line. B Company continued their assault of the initial line. On reaching a sangar containing four of the enemy, Private Percy Wick climbed the side of it. Leaning over the wall he shot three dead and the fourth as he ran away. With the opening assault apparently complete, Horseman and Wick headed to higher ground to fire a Very light flare. This was the prearranged signal for D Company to push through B Company and for the Gurkhas to assault the Afghan centre. As the two men headed off, a depth position opened fire on them. Shotgun pellets wounded Horseman's left shoulder and legs. He got himself up and pushed on with Wick, but a bullet nicked his left ear and he fell-down unconscious.

Private Wick dragged the officer to safety behind a rock, grabbed the Very pistol from him, and then went on to the high ground to obey the order. He was joined by Corporal Arthur Redfern, who crept up and threw a Mills grenade into a depth enemy trench, killing the Afghans in it. He then moved his section round to a flank and threw four grenades at a further trench. Redfern charged with his men, capturing that trench and killing all the occupants. Others in the company amassed on the positions and secured them.

Although successful, the advance and break-in were not without loss for B Company. Private Arthur Chapman and Private William Simpson were both killed, and several others sustained wounds. So, after the first enemy trenches and sangars were cleared and the Very pistol fired, B Company regrouped on the position. D Company pushed through them to clear the line of depth sangars, to which the Afghans in the forward positions had withdrawn. C Company followed close behind. With their fire support now ineffective, A Company manoeuvred around to become the battalion's immediate reserve, echeloning in to the advance behind C Company. But they were not needed, as the three forward companies had captured the enemy's right flank by 10.45 a.m. Once they had reached the line of the ridge, later nicknamed Stafford Ridge, it had taken just fifteen minutes for the battalion to clear out the Afghans. Sadly, during the final clearance, Private John Ware and Private William Ody from C Company were killed.

On the North Staffords' right flank, the 2/11th Gurkhas also succeeded. They advanced over easier ground and, a few minutes after the North Staffords' break-in, burst through the Afghan centre and captured the battery of Afghan guns, bayoneting the gunners. Close behind, exploiting the breakthrough, the 2/123rd Outram's helped secure the ridges. Major General Fowler (1st Division) then ordered the

1/11th Gurkhas to advance and seize Bagh village and the positions at Kafir Kot on the Afghan left flank; which they did with little opposition. By 3 p.m., the brigade had captured the entire objective. It consolidated on it, wary of an Afghan counter-attack and with scant energy left for a pursuit.

With their main positions defeated, the remaining Afghans abandoned the ridges and withdrew in disorder back towards the lower Khyber and out into the Dakka Plain. As they did so, the British mountain batteries caught them with an intensive bombardment, inflicting more Afghan losses. When the retreating enemy moved beyond the range of the artillery, the RAF bombed and machine-gunned them. After, the pilots flew on to attack the Afghan rear at Dakka. As most Afghans had never seen a plane, the material and moral effect of this bombing was significant. The psychological value alone no doubt dissuaded a counter-attack.

Well planned and executed with distinction, the second British attack on the Khargali Ridge, Bagh Springs and Kafir Kot positions was a resounding success. Resolutely beaten, the Afghans were ejected from India by the point of the bayonet. Together, the 2nd Brigade and the other 1st Division units which supported the attack had left over a hundred Afghan dead on the field of battle, with 300 wounded. The brigade had captured two Krupp mountain artillery guns, three pack guns and a machine gun, plus an assortment of rifles, tents, horses, mules and ammunition. But it was a hard-won victory. Anglo-Indian casualties on 11 May totalled eight killed and thirty-one injured. Just over half of these were from the 2nd North Staffords, who lost four killed and suffered eighteen wounded; a mark of the severity of their role in the attack. A few days later, one of the North Staffords wounded – Corporal George Lunt – died of his wounds while undergoing treatment at the hospital in Peshawar. This brought the total North Staffords dead to five.

Without doubt, the successful attack on the Khargali Ridge by the 2nd Brigade was the decisive action of the war. Despite facing a numerically equal force, which was dug-in, with supporting positions and able to fire down on the attacking infantry, the British won the day. With the defeat of the Afghans on their main axis of advance, the British has signalled a message of strength to the 20-30,000 tribesmen in the Khyber area.

The Afghans had not fought badly, but they had fought without initiative. No attempt had been made to concentrate the forces in Ningrahar [in effect, the Dakka Plain], *no attempt had been made to seize Landi Kotal on 6 and 7 May when the British garrison was at its weakest, and most striking of all, no attempt had been made to eject the two British battalions dug-in below the Afghan positions after the action on 9 May. From the British point of view the Landi Kotal situation had the makings of a first-class disaster if the Amir's army had seized the opportunity.*

Putting aside this unexplained Afghan inertia, British success in this critical action was undeniably founded on the North Staffords' proficient assault. Major General Climo recognised this in his brigade commander's message of congratulations, issued soon after the battle:

I thank all ranks, British and Indian, for the devotion to duty and splendid gallantry evinced by them in the action at Khargali, fought over most difficult mountain country and under trying climatic conditions. Especially I wish to express my admiration of the well-ordered, steady attack of The North Staffordshire Regiment, which proceeded like a parade movement. In their gallant assault on their first objective the Battalion secured the key of the position and rendered the further attack on the 11 May possible.

A field signal from the divisional commander Major General Fowler was more succinct:

> *To: O.C. STAFFORDS.*   *Rec.0600 hrs. 12th.*
> *Congratulations to your successful day from Gen. Fowler and please convey his thanks to the troops on their good work.*
> *From: Gen. Staff Suffolk Hill*
> *Time: 1610.*

Later, Commander-in-Chief India, General Sir Charles Monro, picked out the 2nd North Staffords' actions in the Second Battle of Bagh for special mention in his dispatch on the war. The official account of the war by Army Headquarters, India also recognises the prowess of the battalion, commenting on their *'dash and energy'* during the assault. It notes the marked *'keenness of the rank and file'*, recording that each 2nd Brigade battalion had been ordered to leave forty riflemen, back in Landi Kotal. These were to contribute to protecting the fort area during the attack. Some of the battalions complied with this instruction, committing their sick men to the duty. Later, it was found that the North Staffords' nominees had surreptitiously fallen back in with their platoons when they marched off in darkness to the forming-up point, so as not to miss the fight.

With the battle for Khargali Ridge won, Major General Fowler established a line of outposts on the ridge, broadly along the line of the original Afghan positions. These protected the forward elements of the 1st and 2nd brigades, who set up a bivouac camp in and around Bagh village. The wounded were evacuated, and men and animals drew much-needed water from the recaptured springs. Most of the 2nd North Staffords withdrew off the high ground by the late afternoon. A Company remained on the position captured by the battalion to secure it overnight. At dusk, a work party gathered the British dead and buried them in a deep ravine near to the scene of the fighting. Graves were marked by wooden crosses. A thunderstorm during the early evening provided welcome cooling for the exhausted troops. On the morning of 12 May, C Company relieved A Company on the captured position, allowing them to rest for the day. More work parties conducted salvage operations and buried the Afghan dead.

A reconnaissance later in the day found the Afghans still holding the positions at Spin Tsuka, Tor Tsappar and the Ash Khel Ridge. These were fortified with 800 men, the nearest under a mile from Landi Kotal. Brigadier Crocker concluded that there was no advantage in clearing the enemy from these positions. The Afghans were isolated and did not pose a threat to the large British force concentrating at Landi Kotal or at Landi Khana and Bagh. In the meantime, the Afghan force from the Khargali and Kafir Kot ridges had withdrawn to Dakka, eleven miles to the west of Bagh. Once there, they were bombed by the RAF, which panicked them sufficiently that they abandoned much of their equipment and retreated in disorder further west towards Jalalabad.

With the bulk of the British force in the Khyber region now vying for space in the mountain pass, the obvious next step was to cross into Afghanistan. To do this, the British needed to break out to the Dakka Plain. To stay static in Landi Khana and Landi Kotal would have afforded the Afghans the opportunity to regroup and return to the offensive. British inaction or hesitation may have motivated the tribes to support the Amir's call for *jihad*, which would have presented a severe challenge to British supply lines. The plain offered ample space to concentrate sizeable forces and from which the British could advance onto Jalalabad, or even beyond to Kabul.

In view of this, General Monro issued orders from Army

Headquarters for a cavalry force to pursue the Afghans and occupy the Dakka Plain. To support the move, an advance-guard was formed. This included an amalgamated grouping of 160 men from A and D companies of the 2nd North Staffords, commanded by Major S. A. Tuck, the battalion's second-in-command. The composite force deployed during the night of 12/13 May to secure the route west out of the Khyber. Ominously a severe thunderstorm and hail during the early evening accompanied their movement west. The 2/123rd Outram's, with support from a hundred 1/11th Gurkhas established piquets and a transmitting station on hills west of Landi Kotal. These protected the advance-guard's flank from the remaining Afghan positions at Spin Tsuka and Tor Tsappar. By 6 a.m., the forward elements had crossed the frontier at Torkham, a mile from Landi Khana. In doing so, they became the first British troops to enter Afghanistan since 1881. This noteworthy event, along with the capture of the Khargali Ridge, was reported in the first article of the war in *The Times*. The headline read *'British Enter Afghanistan. Strategic Point Seized'*. The story was just two brief paragraphs tucked away on page twelve.

On the approach of the British advance-guard along the main road down from the Khyber, the Afghan troops at the Painda Khak and Haft Chah outposts retreated in haste. At Painda Khak, the North Staffords captured five chests of .303 ammunition. By 10 a.m., the furthest outpost, Haft Chah was in British hands and the route to it piqueted. The entrance to the Dakka Plain was secured, and the route opened for the cavalry. After a short delay, at midday, the 1st Cavalry Brigade passed through and occupied the plain. Unchallenged by the enemy, the first tentative steps into Afghanistan were a success.

Ideally, the advance-guard would have remained in position to keep the route through to the Dakka Plain secure.

But, with insufficient transport to supply the troops beyond Landi Kotal, the divisional headquarters ordered the infantry to pull back. This movement was carried out without contact with either the Afghan regulars or the tribesmen. But, slowed by a severe storm in the late afternoon, the North Staffords' grouping did not make it back up to the bivouac site at Bagh until dusk.

The next day, 14 May, the 1st Brigade headquarters, 1/15th Sikhs, 1/9th Gurkhas and 30th Lancers moved down from the Khyber. They established an infantry brigade presence in Dakka and reinforced the cavalry who were there. At the same time, the enemy at Spin Tsuka, Tor Tsappar and the Ash Khel Ridge were found to have abandoned their positions during the night. Thus, the Afghan invasion ended, at least in the Khyber. The question now became, to what extent would the British pursue their foe into Afghanistan?

CHAPTER FOUR

'On to Jalalabad' (15 May-2 June 1919)

Remaining static at Dakka would achieve little and lay the British open to further attack. So, while the 1st Brigade established a temporary camp, a battalion-sized reconnaissance force left to probe the route out of the plain. On 16 May, the recce troops encountered a force of 3,000 Afghan regulars on their way to recapture Dakka. Over-matched and surprised, the British troops had to fight their way back. Colonel Macmullen, who commanded the action, later described their retirement as *'somewhat uncoordinated and disorganised'*. After heavy fighting, Macmullen ordered a squadron of the 1st King's Dragoon Guards to charge the enemy to avoid the capture of his guns and break contact. This action was the last mounted charge of the British cavalry in the Indian sub-continent. It had the desired effect, and the troops regrouped and extracted back to their main position on the eastern edge of the Dakka Plain.

Spurred on by their initial success, the Afghan regulars pursued the British towards Dakka and then attacked the British lines from the hills around the plain. Exposed and within range of the Afghan guns, Crocker's 1st Brigade struggled to defend itself due to an ill-sited camp. It sustained ten killed and eighty-seven wounded. To regain the initiative, Crocker ordered a night advance and a dawn assault the next day (17 May):

After a preliminary bombardment, the Sikhs attacked but were halted at 8am when ammunition ran out. At 1030am ammunition arrived [with reinforcements from the 3rd Infantry Brigade] *and an attack opened at 2pm in intense heat. After bombardment, the line attacked and reached the top of the deadly escarpment to find that the Afghans had retired leaving equipment, guns and standards.*

After the British had taken the main Afghan positions, later known as Stonehenge Ridge, the rest of their defence collapsed, and they retreated in disorder. By dusk, a British victory was assured but Crocker's troops had narrowly avoided a tactical defeat. British casualties on the second day of the battle were twenty-eight killed and 157 wounded. Afghan losses were 200 killed and 400 wounded, with five guns captured. More significantly, from this point on, the Afghan force ceased to present a credible threat on the Khyber front.

The next sensible move was to pursue the Afghan Army and advance on to Jalalabad, forty miles to the north-west and on a line towards Kabul. Jalalabad was the provincial capital and a key Afghan military base. In a letter to the Secretary of State for India in London, Viscount Chelmsford said that by advancing on Jalalabad '... *we shall by so doing threaten Kabul and force the withdrawal of enemy forces from our frontier'*. But, with the history of failure in the earlier two Anglo-Afghan wars close to mind, an advance needed careful preparation. For that reason, it was decided to stockpile thirty days of supplies at Landi Kotal and Dakka. Once in place, the 1st Cavalry Brigade and the 1st Division would advance to attack Jalalabad. The build-up of troops and supplies was to take two weeks, and the force aimed to be ready to move by early June.

*****

Since the early 1880s, the British Army had assigned the security of the Khyber Pass to the Khyber Rifles. Locally recruited from Afridi tribesmen, the British-officered unit secured the Pass from the border with Afghanistan to Landi Kotal, where they were headquartered. From Landi Kotal it provided security down to Ali Masjid and onto Jamrud Fort to the east. It was an important task, as the route was a single road dominated in many stretches by hills coming down close on either side. It required piqueting all the way to protect convoys from being attacked by tribesmen on the heights above them. But, as the Third Afghan War began, there was a mass of desertions from the Khyber Rifles and a decision was taken to disband them. In their place a defence and security force, known as Defsec, was formed. Led by the 3rd Infantry Brigade's commander, Major General A. Skeen, it maintained lines of communication between Landi Kotal and the forward troops on the Dakka Plain. Protection of the eastern Khyber Pass from Landi Kotal down to Jamrud Fort was assigned to the 2nd Division, who had now moved up into the Khyber from their base in Rawalpindi. Instead of heading into Afghanistan, the bulk of the 2nd Brigade were allocated to the Defsec command. This subordination included the 2nd North Staffords, who moved down from Bagh to Landi Khana on 14 May, where they co-located with the 2nd Brigade's headquarters. A perimeter camp was quickly established, and this became the battalion's home for the rest of the war.

From their base at Landi Khana, the Defsec units took

turns securing the area around the camp and providing temporary piquets along the route west to Dakka. These extended as far as Haft Chah, an old Afghan fort near Torkham on the border. Beyond there the 1st Brigade troops maintained a system of permanent piquets up to their camp on the Dakka Plain. Defsec's piquets comprised a line on the hills covering the western and southern approaches to Landi Khana and a second line which provided over-watch along the Dakka road.

A piquet sangar was roughly oval, formed by constructing a dry stonewall. This afforded the piquet party, typically made up of a non-commissioned officer and six to thirty men, a degree of protection while posted on the exposed hilltops. The walls were often built to around a metre-and-a-half high, which allowed the defending troops to stand upright and fire over them. Loopholes were incorporated at ground level to counter any close assault of the piquets. On the rare occasions that a piquet had a Lewis machine gun, a nest would be built at either end of the sangar to accommodate this. Supplies, medical equipment and signalling devices were kept in the centre of the sangar. Ground sheets stretched inwards from the walls to give protection from the sun. Normally, the piquets would be occupied during daylight hours, with troops withdrawing to Landi Khana after the daily convoys to Dakka had passed through.

On occasion, more piqueting was needed to respond to increased enemy threats. On 17 May, for example, the 2nd North Staffords' second-in-command took half of the battalion to piquet the heights overlooking the Dakka Road. Concurrently, Lieutenant Colonel Fox took the other half forward to the Afghan outpost at Haft Chah. They were acting as an advance-guard for the 3rd Infantry Brigade, which then marched through them to reinforce the British attack at Dakka the same day.

Besides piqueting, the North Staffords adopted a form of routine. Inspections were conducted and fatigue parties carried out daily cleaning chores, improved the camp perimeter and strengthened the piquet sangars. Periodically, reconnaissance patrols checked for enemy activity. Physical training sessions were held, Lewis gun drills were practised, field firing conducted, and lectures were given to subalterns and non-commissioned officers on mountain warfare. Over time, bivouac tents were replaced with improved E.P. (English Privates) camp tents and new field service rations were introduced. These added luxuries such as condensed milk, fruit and sweets to the soldiers' diets. Medical parades took place daily and a constant stream of sick men moved to and from rear locations for treatment and to recuperate. Heatstroke, sanitation-related illnesses and sand fly fever were common conditions. Cholera was less common at Landi Khana, owing to the ready access to clean water from the Bagh Springs. Over time, a rudimentary leave rota was established, with small groups of men returning to Nowshera for a short period.

*****

While the Amir's main effort had been to take control of the Khyber Pass and advance through to Peshawar, the Afghan Army advanced on two other primary fronts; into Waziristan from Khost and, further south, into Balochistan via the Chaman border. The advance from Khost, seventy miles south of the Khyber, ended up splitting into separate fronts in North and South Waziristan. A hundred miles north of the Pass there was a minor Afghan thrust into the Chitral. Fighting also occurred in the Zhob, which links Waziristan and Balochistan. The theatre of operations was vast, with the five or six fronts extending over 800 miles along the Indo-

Afghan border. Across these fronts there were successes and failures on both sides, and a few sizeable actions.

Principally, the British campaign plan was to keep an active defence on these other fronts, reserving its main striking capacity for the Jalalabad-Khyber axis. As a result, General Monro directed that preparations be made to evacuate positions in the tribal area between the administrative border and the actual border with Afghanistan. He aimed to reduce the risk to the detachments in those areas, while avoiding any embarrassing commitments. The tactic also allowed him to concentrate as large a force as possible at the decisive point on the Khyber line. This course of action was bolstered by increasing concerns that the frontier militias would desert.

On 21 May, a few days after the Afghan counter-attack at Dakka had been blunted, further intelligence was received. It reported that General Nadir Khan was intending to advance with the central Afghan force into Waziristan, via either the Tochi or Kurram valleys. Khan had been the Afghan Commander-in-Chief at the time of Amir Habibullah's murder. Expecting the frontier militia and limited regular troops to be over-matched, the withdrawal from certain militia posts was ordered. When he heard of the abandonment of the posts, the Chief Commissioner of the North-West Frontier Province, Sir George Roos-Keppel, was furious. He foresaw the unintended consequence of accelerating desertions from the North and South Waziristan Militia, and that it would encourage the local tribes to support the Afghan cause. This prediction was proved true almost immediately. When the militia post at Wana in South Waziristan was abandoned on 26 May, the British officers that led them – together with 300 loyal men – had to fight their way out. Some were massacred by agitated tribesmen before they could escape. Famously, the officer in charge, Major Guy

Hamilton Russell, led a sixty-mile fighting evacuation over five days to reach the safety of British lines at Fort Sandeman. He was heralded as the hero of the war. With the conditions now favourable for an advance, Nadir Khan's fourteen battalions crossed the border on 24 May, supported by thirty-six guns and swelling numbers of tribesmen. They entered Waziristan by three separate routes, diluting the ability of the British forces to respond.

The immediate results were disastrous for the British. A joint force of Afghan regulars and 12,000 tribesmen headed first for the (abandoned) militia post at Spinwam, capturing it with ease. Next, on 27 May, they attacked the British fort and camp at Thal which guarded the Kurram Pass. Thal was defended by just four under-strength battalions of Sikhs and Gurkhas, and a squadron of cavalry. In their initial attack, the Afghans destroyed the fort's food dumps. Outnumbered, out-gunned and with few supplies, the British force was in serious trouble. Thal looked set to fall. After four days it was saved by a relief force from Peshawar led by Brigadier Reginald E. H. Dyer, fresh from his notorious actions at Amritsar to suppress the Punjab rebellion. Dyer's troops arrived on 31 May and helped the defenders turn the tide. They forced the withdrawal of the Afghans back to their own territory. While the attack was ongoing, a party of Afghans approached Dyer's headquarters under a flag of truce. They delivered a message that the Amir had ordered Nadir Khan to suspend hostilities. Nadir Khan asked for an acknowledgement. Dyer, who did not know of the truce, gave the answer, *'My guns will give you an immediate reply, but your letter will be forwarded to the Divisional Commander'*. The attack continued until the Afghans withdrew. Dyer then ordered the 37th Lancers and his armoured cars to pursue and harass the enemy. On 3 June, his small force seized the Afghan camp at Yusef Khel which had provide a mounting base for Nadir

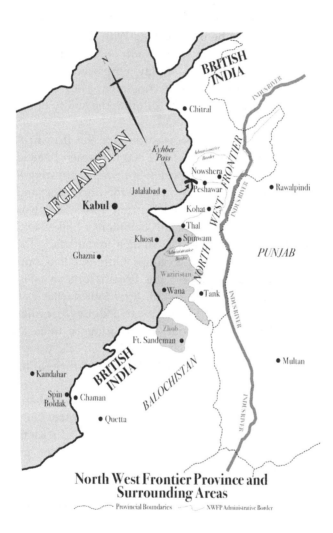

North West Frontier Province and Surrounding Areas

.... Provincial Boundaries ⌐⌐⌐ NWFP Administrative Border

Khan's advance.

After the relief of Thal in early June, there was a reorganisation of the troops in the Kohat-Kurram area. This included the formation of the 65th Brigade, led by Brigadier Charles Tanner. Temporarily promoted to command the brigade, Tanner was a former North Staffords officer. In response to continued sniping and low-level attacks, the 65th Brigade carried out attacks against the Waziri tribes south of Thal through to the end of the war.

Operations in Waziristan's Kurram area were commanded by Brigadier Edward A. Fagan, a (late) South Staffordshire Regiment officer. During the defence of Thal, a smaller Afghan force of 2–3,000 regulars had crossed the border to invade the Upper Kurram. They were backed up by 1-2,000 tribesmen and were facing off the loyal militia force there, in and around Kharlachi. After a stand-off and small contacts, Fagan's force attacked the Afghans on 2 June. They captured Kharlachi and destroyed six hostile villages. Other successful minor operations followed, quashing the Afghan attempt to break through on the Kurram front. Military historian Brian Robson has praised Fagan's leadership. He commented that although Fagan *'had been fortunate in his subordinates, he had nevertheless shown himself to be a courageous and competent commander. It would be hard to find a better conducted small campaign than that fought in the Upper Kurram.'*

Despite this success and other operations in central and southern Waziristan, the area remained a hotbed of activity throughout the war. The Waziris were one of the few tribes to respond in force to the Amir's call to rise against the British. A difficult insurgency campaign followed. The fighting in late 1919 and into 1920 was the most serious ever fought on the frontier. Roos-Keppel captured the situation when he wrote that *'Amanullah has lit a fire that will take us a great deal of trouble to put out'*. At certain times during the later campaign, the

British almost faced a humiliating defeat. The Waziristan Campaign did not conclude until mid-1920.

Between Waziristan and Baluchistan, in the Zhob, the Afghans achieved initial minor successes, aided by the Waziris and other tribes. One of these attacks, involved Captain Reginald Copland another North Staffords officer. He had served with the 5th Battalion in France during the First World War. After the war he was posted to India on attachment to the 3rd Battalion 1st King George's Own Gurkha Rifles (The Malaun Regiment). On the 16 July, he was commanding a relief force of 225 men and a section of guns sent to aid a convoy. The convoy, operating in the Fort Sandeman area of the Upper Zhob, had been attacked by a modest Waziri *lashkar* and needed an escort to get it home. After the relief force had linked up with the convoy, they set off back, and reached Kapip, ten miles east of Fort Sandeman, without incident. Then, as the troops cautiously approached a defile, the *lashkar* attacked again, and with a much larger force. Ahead of the small British convoy, on the hills above the defile, were 2,000 tribesmen.

Captain Copland... sent forward two parties, one under Lieutenant Dobbin... and one under Lieutenant ffrench to clear the hills overlooking the defile and post piquets on them. These attacks were supported by artillery fire, but they only succeeded in establishing themselves on the lower spurs. The enemy then began to press the flanks and on the rear of the column. The convoy was advanced a few hundred yards close up behind the advanced guard. The enemy poured in a heavy fire from the hills and inflicted many casualties on men and animals. The advanced guard was unable to make further progress in spite of one gun being run up almost level with them. Captain Copland then went forward with all the men he could collect, which amounted to about twenty, but he found it impossible to make any headway, and was forced to retire after his party suffered many casualties. The men were now utterly exhausted after the hard piqueting and fighting in which they had already been engaged. Captain Copland, however, managed to scrape together another small party with which he endeavoured to advance, but he was killed in the attempt.

Soon after, Lieutenant Dobbin and Lieutenant ffrench were both killed. Faced with a charge of the convoy by the tribesmen in overwhelming numbers, the remaining troops were over-powered and fierce hand-to-hand fighting ensued. As nightfall came, the one surviving British officer, a young second lieutenant, ordered the convoy to be abandoned. The guns were disabled and the troops scattered, making their way back to Fort Sandeman in twos and threes. By the end of the engagement, one of the deadliest and disastrous of the war, fifty-three British or Indian men had been killed and seventy-one wounded. The dead were left on the battlefield. There were other tribesmen-led attacks in the Zhob, but Fort Sandeman remained in British hands and the Afghans did not exploit the opportunities created by their tribal brethren.

Further south, in Balochistan, the British took the fight to the enemy. The commander there seized the initiative by conducting a cross-border operation to capture the Afghan fort at Spin Boldak. This outpost was close to the British position at Chaman and served as a screen behind which the enemy could have concentrated to attack Chaman or the British flank. It also guarded the strategically vital road from Kandahar to Quetta. A successful assault, against a fortress which the Afghans didn't adequately reinforce, was carried out on 27 May. It was notable as the last time the British Army used an escalade. Two hundred of the 500 Afghans defending Spin Boldak were killed. After this attack, operations in the southern front were largely settled.

North of the Khyber, in the Chitral, the Afghans advanced

across the border on 12 May and occupied the Indian town of Arnawai. In several battles, the Chitral Scouts militia and a small mobile column of regular troops attacked the Afghans and – by 23 May – had driven them back over the border. Later, in June, the Chitralis conducted several retribution raids into Afghanistan.

Back in the Khyber, operations focused on maintaining secure lines of communications. On 15 and 16 May, the 6th Infantry Brigade carried out operations near Ali Masjid and inflicted heavy casualties on the enemy. North of Peshawar, on 20 May, Afghan regulars crossed into the administrative area and headed towards Shabkadr, supported by a *lashkar* of Mohmand tribesmen. There were echoes here of the battles fought by the 2nd North Staffords around Shabkadr in 1915. A brigade from the 16th Division and judicious bombing raids by the RAF forced the Afghans to retire.

A week later, on 24 May, the RAF had another notable success. This was when a lone Handley Page V/1500 bomber crewed by Captain Robert 'Jock' Halley RAF, with an observer and three sergeants, delivered a daring aerial attack on Kabul. Given the elevations and distance involved, the sortie was a remarkable achievement. Its success lay in a convenient east wind that blew the aircraft over the Spin Ghar mountains to get it to Kabul. It fortuitously then changed course to blow it back again. The bombs themselves did little damage. But, the appearance of this *'flying machine'* over the Kabul skies was important in producing a desire for peace at the headquarters of the Afghan Government.

CHAPTER FIVE

An Armistice But No Peace
(3 June-8 August 1919)

Whatever the true rationale for the war, it quickly became clear that Amanullah lacked the resolve to continue with hostilities. After the repulse of his Khyber advance, the defeat of the Dakka counter-attack, and the failed uprising in Peshawar, the Amir made tentative moves towards peace. RAF attacks on Jalalabad and Captain 'Jock' Halley's bombing on the Afghan capital Kabul solidified the Amanullah's decision. On 28 May, he wrote to the Viceroy requesting peace.

Despite the likelihood of a British victory, the Indian Government was keen to end the war.

The army... had coped admirably with the conflict [but]*... the strain was beginning to tell. Men and machines were beginning to run down, transport and supplies were beginning to exert an increasing strain and the Commander-in-Chief... was already warning that if the war continued much longer, resources available in India might be inadequate.*

A widespread outbreak of cholera along the frontier was

threatening to overwhelm medical resources. Furthermore, the British Government was *'resolutely opposed to going all the way to Kabul and keen to avoid an entanglement, believing it would take more troops than were in the whole of India to occupy Afghanistan effectively'*.

On receiving the Amir's letter on 3 June, Viscount Chelmsford, not wishing to prejudice the overture for peace, halted the planned advance on Jalalabad. He then ordered an immediate ceasefire. Confirmation of the armistice quickly cascaded down to the Afghan troops in the Khyber. A day later a small group of them approached the 2nd North Staffords' lines bearing a white flag. But, despite British hopes for a swift end to the war, the Amir played a long game, delaying his officials from attending the peace talks by almost two months. The first month of this delay coincided with Ramadan, the ninth month of the Islamic calendar. In this period of religious observance most Afghans would have fasted during daylight hours, giving them a subdued appetite for fighting. Amanullah may have considered that it was worth holding back on the peace talks, hoping for a tribal uprising after Ramadan ended on 29 June.

Because of Ramadan, or the Amir's genuine interest in a concord, the Afghan regulars maintained peaceful dispositions during June. On the other hand, *'in spite of the armistice conditions, Afghan officials were everywhere busy endeavouring to incite the tribesmen to rise'* and achieved success in doing so. Many tribal *lashkars* formed, some estimated to be several thousand tribesmen strong. These threatened forts, camps and entire piquet lines, while smaller groups kept the Anglo-Indian troops active through constant sniping and small raids, mainly at night. Individual piquets were the target of these attacks or, as the outer layer of defence for main positions or routes, were the first to identify and contact the enemy.

DETAIL OF PIQUETS

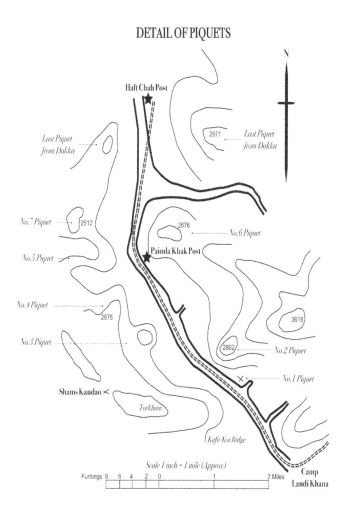

N

Haft Chah Post

2971

Last Piquet
from Dakka

Last Piquet
from Dakka

No. 7 Piquet   2512

2676

No. 6 Piquet

No. 5 Piquet

Painda Khak Post

No. 4 Piquet

2676

3618

No. 3 Piquet

2802

No. 2 Piquet

No. 1 Piquet

Shams Kandao

Torkham

Kafir Kot Ridge

Camp
Landi Khana

Scale 1 inch = 1 mile (Approx)

Furlongs 8   6   4   2   0   1   2 Miles

On the Khyber front, Major General Skeen ordered the British cavalry at Dakka to carry out two ambushes. These were on parties of Mohmands and Shinwaris and were designed to deter the harassment of his forces. They took place on 19 and 20 June and were successful, but led the Shinwari leader, Zar Shah, to conduct a revenge attack. He chose to ambush a piquet near Landi Khana on 22 June.

On that day, the piqueting force of 215 men was provided by the 2nd North Staffords. Led by Captain C. R. P. Hearn (OC D Company), the force had left camp at sunrise to occupy the piquets overlooking the road to Dakka. The first four piquets of seven were posted without trouble. Ahead of moving the final three piquets, Nos. 4, 5 and 7, into position, two reserve platoons were positioned in the valley below them. By 6.45 a.m., No. 4 piquet had taken up its position and No. 7 piquet had reached a point halfway up the hill they were to occupy.

Leading No. 5 piquet was Second Lieutenant S. Harris, who then went forward of the main party with his sergeant to recce the occupation of his piquet. No enemy were observed. But, as his piquet topped the crest of the hill on which it was to be sited, the leading line of six men came under heavy fire. A group of Shinwari tribesmen, estimated to be forty to fifty in strength, were in concealed firing positions a hundred metres away across open flat ground. The opening volley of the ambush killed two soldiers and severely wounded three. A sixth man narrowly avoided injury when a shot passed through his Wolseley pith helmet but missed his head. In the ensuing firefight, No. 5 piquet managed to suppress the enemy while they reorganised themselves. Under a hail of bullets, medic Private C. J. Monro RAMC bravely dressed the bullet wounds of the three injured soldiers. Meanwhile, the piquet's signaller, Private J. N. Bloor, relayed vital messages about the contact back to Captain Hearn. He did this despite being subjected to heavy enemy fire every time he waved his signalling flags.

Although taken by surprise, the piqueting force was well placed to react. Covering parties immediately opened fire, utilising the high rate of fire of the Lewis guns to regain the initiative. The rest of No. 5 piquet then moved off to the right flank and attacked the enemy up a reverse slope from the north-west. OC A Company, Lieutenant E. L. G. Beville, moved up ten men from the reserve force still on the Dakka road to counter-attack up a south-easterly spur. At this point, facing attack from multiple directions, the enemy withdrew from their ambush position towards the south-east. Just before they did, Lieutenant Beville was shot, but his injuries were not life-threatening. No. 4 piquet, in position to the south, then engaged the enemy. It forced them back in front of No. 5 piquet, who had now formed a baseline, and then continued their forward movement to clear them from the ridge. Eventually, the tribesmen were forced to shelter on a hill feature out of range to the infantry weapons. They were finally evicted by shells from a section of No. 6 (Mountain) Battery RGA which had been dispatched from Landi Khana as soon as trouble was reported. By the end of the contact, sixteen enemy had been killed, with others wounded. The remainder fled westwards.

It took over three hours to conclude the follow-up, but the North Staffords sustained no further casualties. By 8 a.m., all the piquets had been posted. As a precaution, the section of howitzers remained in support for the rest of the day and a cavalry squadron swept the area to which the Afghans had withdrawn. In mid-afternoon, the commanding officer and a hundred other ranks came forward to cover the piqueting forces' withdrawal. The tribesmen did not reappear, and all the troops had returned safely to camp by 8 p.m. Those soldiers killed in the ambush were Private Alfred Payne and

Private Alfred Matthews. Two of the injured soldiers, Acting Sergeant James Ryan and Private John Malpass, also later died, despite the medic's efforts to save them. The four dead were buried at Landi Kotal Cemetery. Lieutenant Beville and the other wounded soldier, Private Forman, were evacuated to Landi Khana and recovered.

This incident is recorded in the official account of the war as:

...a good example of troops at a disadvantage extricating themselves by their own courage and initiative. The covering fire was well organised, and ready when it was required. The Lewis gun and rifle shooting was good. This, combined with the promptness with which the piquet changed the direction of the attack while still continuing to advance, converted an awkward situation into a creditable victory.

It was to have repercussions throughout the British force, as temporary piqueting was abandoned after the attack and replaced by a system of permanent piquets.

The last week of June passed without incident for the battalion. Reinforcements trickled in, fatigue parties strengthened the sangars in the piquets and camp, and detachments escorted supplies down from Landi Kotal. Cleaning parades and inspections were held, field firing training was conducted, sick and wounded were moved out, and a lucky few rotated onto leave. Back in Europe, on 28 June, the Paris Peace Conference concluded, and the Treaty of Versailles was signed. Although welcome news in India, this formal end to the First World War had little impact on the North-West Frontier. There, the British still waited for the start of the peace conference for the Third Afghan War.

Into July and still without sign of an Afghan peace delegation, piquets continued and were persistently attacked up and down the frontier. One such incident, on 9 July, resulted in another fatality for the North Staffords – but not a human one. Second Lieutenant A. B. Savory, who had joined the battalion midway through their deployment, was commanding a platoon on Khargali Ridge when they were ambushed soon after sunset. The 2nd North Staffords' war diary records details of the contact:

At 1850 the piquet at KHARGALI S. was fired on by a party of Raiders about 45 strong from E slopes of Hill Point 4596. Enemy were well concealed in sangars nearest sniper being about 500^x from the piquet. Fire was opened by L.G. [Lewis Gun] and E. slope of hill searched range to crest of hill 1100^x it was presumed a few casualties were obtained owing to darkness coming on this could not be verified. At 1910, both piquets were fired on from the way of KHARGALI Village. L.G. fire was brought to bear on the S corner of village and point 4596 immediately after the enemy were seen making their way in twos and threes towards the village.

Fortunately for the newly arrived Second Lieutenant Savory, the Khargali South piquet was under the charge of Sergeant Redfern. He had been promoted in the field after his distinguished actions in the Second Battle of Bagh. Thirty minutes after the initial contact, the piquets were reached by a hundred-strong body of reinforcements from Landi Khana under the command of Captain Hatton. The situation stabilised. Individual piquets were bolstered with other riflemen and there was no further sniping during the night. The robust response sent a further message to the tribesmen that the North Staffords were a professional regular army force that would fight back with tenacity. The dead comrade killed in the ambush was Private Line, a Supply and Transport mule which had been carrying supplies for the piquets. Line was one of 158,000 animals used to carry the men and equipment of the British Indian Army during the war.

After this unfortunate incident, July passed quietly for the battalion. There were only two other sniping attacks that month, despite occasional intelligence reports of potential attacks on Landi Khana by larger enemy groups. In Dakka, on the Afghan side of the border, the harassment of the British occupiers was more pronounced, with small *lashkars* attacking on 5, 12 and 23 July. Events eight miles south of the Khyber Pass also threatened to overturn the armistice. On 18 July, a *lashkar* of 10,000 tribesmen gathered in the Bazar Valley and attacked the standing piquet line from there to Ali Masjid Fort at multiple points. A determined defence combined with aerial bombing dispersed the tribesmen. Remarkably, on the same day, the North Staffords were permitted a day off. This was to celebrate the official end to the First World War, twenty days after the Versailles treaty had been signed. A free issue of beer or rum was given to each man, though the celebrations were muted owing to the lack of progress towards concluding peace on the frontier.

British patience with the Amir for not sending a delegation to begin peace talks came to a head in mid-July. At this point the Viceroy sent Amanullah a final summons for a delegation to be dispatched. He wrote that:

The Amir seems to forget it was the Afghan Government that began the war and is now suing for peace, nor does the Amir realise that His Majesty's Government have been very gravely affronted by what has occurred and that the British people are indignant that a great power should thus have been wantonly attacked.

It was not just the Indian Government that were riled by the Amir's deliberate temporising. As with the rest of the British troops, the North Staffords' men were frustrated by the delay.

Some relief came when the battalion watched the Afghan peace delegates pass through their lines on 24 July. An end to the tedium and discomfort of piquet duties looked to be in sight. It took a further day for the Afghan delegation to arrive in Rawalpindi, with the peace conference starting on 26 July. Even during these negotiations, sniping at British piquets continued. War diary entries for the 2nd North Staffords reported one of these at the end of July and a further two in early August:

28/29th July 0115 hrs
Halt. Battalion on Road piquets. At the time stated a few shots were fired on KAFFIR KOT W piquets from the direction of KHARGALI Village. The Camp xx was also sniped from the vicinity of Torkham at 0115 hrs no casualties.

1st August   2250 hrs
Sniping occurred during the night 1 & 2 August at 2250 to 2310 from the TORKHAM Ridge. No casualties.

5th August   0830 hrs
Halt. Battalion on Road piquets sniping took place from the direction of TORKHAM about 0830 hrs. Casualties Nil.

Frustratingly, a fourth incident led to the wounding of a North Staffords soldier:

7th August
Halt. Battalion on KHARGALI piquets. At 1830 piquets were fired on by snipers from Point No. 4597 distance 1100^x normal conditions at 1840. Casualties Pte. LOVEYS D Coy. Slightly wounded. Remainder of the night was quiet.

After two weeks of talks, terms were agreed, and a peace

treaty was signed on 8 August. Hoping generous terms would bring stability to the North-West Frontier, the British agreed to recognise Afghan control of its external affairs. This gave Afghanistan the independence that Amanullah had requested from the British in March and that his late father had requested at the end the First World War. In return, the Afghans agreed that the Durand Line be properly recognised as the permanent border between Afghanistan and India. The peace terms ended the British subsidy to the Amir and forbid the importation of arms and ammunition through India. Besides these, it imposed no territorial losses or financial reparations upon Afghanistan. Accordingly, the treaty was hailed as a victory in Kabul and led *The Times* to observe that the Afghans had *'unquestionably won the peace and so the war'*.

Nonetheless, the Treaty of Rawalpindi and the later treaty of perpetual friendship – signed in Kabul in 1921 – enabled the British to look forward to peaceful coexistence with Afghanistan. Moreover *'the speed with which the British forces had mobilised and crushed the Afghans made it clear that the British were not about to surrender India and that Indian independence, when it came, would not be won by military means'*.

Although the Treaty of Rawalpindi was signed in early August 1919, it took several weeks for the British to extract from Afghan territory. The immediate change for the 2nd North Staffords was a short move from their camp at Landi Khana back to Bagh, where they carried out local defence. Once there, the battalion's routine changed little. They continued to man piquets, although there was a marked decrease in tribal activity. Inevitably, the battalion got involved in hosting and supporting the visits of various dignitaries. The divisional commander received a tour of the Khargali Ridge action and Viscount Chelmsford passed through the lower Khyber on route to visit troops at Dakka.

In early September, British forces withdrew from Dakka,

which they accomplished without loss. On 6 September, just shy of a month after the peace signing, the 2nd North Staffords were relieved from their piquet duties by the 2/54 Sikhs. From Bagh, the battalion of sixteen officers and 379 other ranks marched out of the Khyber Pass, through Ali Masjid to the railhead at Jamrud. Once there, they boarded trains back to their peacetime location at Khartoum Barracks in Nowshera. The battalion arrived home on 9 September after four months on operations, having seen their main action within five days of their deployment.

*****

In his official report on the Third Afghan War, General Monro (Commander-in-Chief India) praised all involved:

I… [commend]… the fine military spirit in which the troops accepted the burden of this campaign; this spirit was fully maintained in the field, and all ranks, British and Indian, showed themselves to be animated by the determination to close with the enemy which is the surest guarantee of success. No greater testimony of this spirit could be adduced than the cheerfulness with which all ranks endured the trying climatic conditions prevailing and the discomforts inevitable in the opening stages of a campaign.

For their efforts, officers and soldiers who served in the war earned the India General Service Medal (1908-1935) with the 'Afghanistan N.W.F. 1919' clasp. The actions of individuals were also recognised. Within the 2nd North Staffords, Corporal A. Redfern and Private P. Wick were conferred the Distinguished Conduct Medal (DCM) for their actions at the Second Battle of Bagh. For other ranks, this medal for distinguished, gallant and good conduct in the field was second only to the Victoria Cross for gallantry. No Victoria

Crosses were awarded for the Third Afghan War and just seven DCMs were conferred across the whole force. In addition, Redfern and Wick were Mentioned in Dispatches. Captain F. Hatton and Second Lieutenant E. Horseman were awarded the Military Cross for the gallantry they demonstrated leading the forward elements of the same attack. Lieutenant Colonel E. Fox was awarded the Distinguished Service Order (DSO) for distinguished services during active operations against the enemy. Company Quartermaster Sergeants R. Barker and W. Evans earned the Meritorious Service Medal for acts of gallantry not in the presence of the enemy. Four other men serving with the battalion were Mentioned in Dispatches. These were Captain E. A. Squirrell (Adjutant), Company Sergeant-Major E. G. Fogg, Corporal G. Lakin and Private J. M. Bloor. The latter two commendations were for their actions during the piquet attack on 22 June. Three further North Staffords men were Mentioned in Dispatches. These were Colonel (temporary Brigadier) C. O. Tanner, who led 65th Brigade in the Kurram area, Sergeant B. H. Philpot and Sergeant (temporary) W. G. Jones. The two sergeants were attached to other units during the fighting. Brigadier E. A. Fagan (late South Staffords) was made a Companion of the Most Exalted Order of the Star of India for his leadership of 60th Brigade.

The battalion's contribution to the Third Afghan War was further recognised by the award of the battle honour 'Afghanistan N.W.F. 1919'. It was the last of sixty honours awarded to the Prince of Wales's (North Staffordshire) Regiment during the First World War and its immediate aftermath. Later, it was chosen by the wider regiment to be one of ten battle honours awarded during the 1914-1919 period that were added to the regiment's Colours.

With the Third Afghan War concluded, the long-awaited demobilisation of British and Indian troops commenced in earnest. After the volunteers and conscripts in the North Staffords had received their orders to ship home to England, only fifteen officers and around 150 men remained in India. The battalion itself then received orders to leave India. Re-titled the 2nd Battalion The North Staffordshire Regiment (The Prince of Wales's), it left the North-West Frontier on 17 January 1920. It moved first to Egypt, arriving there a month later, where it was reinforced with remnants of a service battalion. At that point, Colonel Fox (newly promoted) who had led the battalion since October 1914, handed over command to Major Tweedie. The battalion then headed south for a year of colonial duties in Anglo-Egyptian Sudan. It finally returned home to Lichfield, Staffordshire in 1921.

CHAPTER SIX

Reflections

H. G. Wells' phrase *'the war to end war'* proffered a vision that the First World War would relegate war to history. The term was already being used sardonically by the time of the armistice and any lingering hopes for perpetual peace were mis-founded. Even before the guns fell silent over the battlefields of the Western Front, other wars had surfaced, stimulated by the turmoil created by the world war. So, in 1919, the British military found itself fighting alongside the White Russians against the Bolsheviks in the Russian Civil War. It also supported wars of independence in Estonia, Latvia, Turkey and – closer to home – in Ireland. Like these, the Third Afghan War was a reaction against the old-world order.

Given the calls for independence against the British, Russian, Turkish and other empires, it is surprising that the British and Indian governments misunderstood the Afghan situation so profoundly. The administrations knew of Afghan grievances but, because of both ignorance and arrogance, they concluded that the threat was not serious; at least not sufficiently so to induce the Afghans to take offensive action. Therefore, the invasion took the British by surprise.

A cross-border assault was a bold move by the Amir and one probably founded on securing his own political position rather than any serious attempt to capture territory. Yet, given India's fragile socio-economic position at the time and an Anglo-Indian military amid a messy post-war transition, the invasion did have a chance of success. It failed, for the most part, due to the Afghan military's poor planning, inept coordination and badly led military operations. Critically, the Amir did not adequately synchronise actions on the different fronts. The Khyber advance was premature and took place three weeks before the Waziristan and Kurram advances. It took even longer for the Afghans to reach the southern border region, allowing the British to seize the initiative at Spin Boldak. Above all, the invasion of India relied on a general uprising of the frontier tribes which, luckily for the British, failed to materialise. Tribal *lashkars* did form, but less for those in Waziristan, they did not present a difficult challenge.

The Amir's miscalculation and the swift defeat of the Afghan military are not reasons to discount the Third Afghan War as irrelevant. Had the British not responded with speed and scale, the outcome of the war may not have been assured. Although surprised, the British got troops up into the Khyber before the Afghans could bolster their advance-guard. Alongside this initial reaction, the British and Indian forces mobilised and launched a massive land and air campaign to defend the frontier; the force applied likened by some historians *'to hitting a mosquito with a sledgehammer'*. Testing its beleaguered post-world war resources to the full, the Army deployed eight divisions to fight the Afghans, with another two in reserve; albeit just 75,000 of these were fighting troops and no action ever used more than the equivalent of two brigades. A lesser response may still have succeeded but would almost certainly have resulted in the loss of the Khyber. This would have emboldened frontier tribes, enabled

Afghan regulars to break out of the mountains, and may have fired up an insurrection throughout India.

The war was further noteworthy because of the distances over which the operations were conducted, with multiple fronts spread over 800 miles. Also, it employed the advanced technology that had emerged from the First World War, such as the armoured car, motor transport, machine guns and aircraft. These were used in more manoeuvrist ways than had been possible on the Western Front. But, at the same time, the Third Afghan War had many of the features of a standard frontier campaign, with older tactics such as escalade attacks and the cavalry charge used. The official account remembers it for the intensity and impact of several cholera outbreaks, which were '*the most extensive and sudden that have occurred in frontier warfare; at one time they threatened to immobilise the Forces*', the failure of the system of tribal militias, and the abnormal severe heat endured by the troops.

Deaths in war are lamentable, but especially in this war, which was seemingly more pointless than most. Mercifully, for both sides, the casualty rate was low compared with the First World War. The three months of frontier war were broadly equal to those of a quiet day on the Western Front. Afghan military casualties are recorded as 600 killed and 1,000 wounded. British and Indian casualties were roughly half of these, with 236 killed in action and 615 wounded. Additionally, there were 57,000 sickness cases across the British force, of which 900 died, mainly from cholera. In India, the most notable memorial to those who died is the Delhi Memorial (India Gate). It is dedicated:

To the dead of the Indian Armies who fell honoured in France and Flanders Mesopotamia and Persia East Africa Gallipoli and elsewhere in the near and far-east and in sacred memory also of those who names are recorded and who fell in India and the North-

West Frontier and during the Third Afghan War.

The 1914-1918 War Memorial in Karachi, Pakistan also commemorates those who served and died in the Afghan war.

Reflecting on the war, historian Brian Robson wrote that although:

...viewed from the distance of time, the Third Anglo-Afghan War must appear to have been one of the most absurd and unnecessary wars that Britain (and India) has ever been involved in... [It] gave each of the combatants what they wanted – for the Afghans full independence and, for the British, a fixed frontier and the prospect of a permanent peace. The tragedy was that neither objective required a war to achieve it.

Despite this, the Third Afghan War was a noble victory for the British Indian Army. They did suffer a few minor reverses in the field, sustained at the hands of the tribesmen. But, these were due principally to the wide extent of the front of operations, poor communications, the shortage of experienced officers and the rawness of many of the British troops. Less for an occasional stalled attack, an ambush of a small force, or a temporary withdrawal, the Afghan regular troops were defeated every time they were encountered.

Setting this aside, the war should be remembered most for leading Afghanistan to be the first British protectorate, colony or dominion to achieve independence after the First World War. In Afghanistan the Third Afghan War is known as the War of Independence. And, the country still marks their release from British control with annual Roz-e Peroz-e Afġānestān (independence day) celebrations on the anniversary of the Treaty of Rawalpindi. The treaty cemented the beginning of the end of the British Empire, which started its steady decline after the onset of the world war in 1914. Over sixty territories have since ceded from the empire. While we cannot attribute this wave of nationalism to the Afghans, they led the way; confirming it was possible to challenge Great Britain and succeed politically, without winning militarily.

And what of the contribution by the 2nd North Staffords? Throughout the North-West Frontier Campaign and the Third Afghan War, they certainly maintained their high reputation for tough fighting ability and for being *'a fine shooting battalion'*. A 1923 history of the regiment recorded that:

The two campaigns in which the 2nd North Staffords had taken part during their stay in India were on a small scale compared with the fighting which had taken place in Europe, but anyone familiar with that inhospitable district known as the North-West Frontier of India will realise the difficulties, both of terrain and climate, with which they had to contend. The Battalion had not only cheerfully endured the boredom and suffering inevitable on active service, especially in that part of the world, but also had on at least two occasions attacked and beaten an enemy acknowledged to be most expert hill fighters, and that in their own country, wherein every rock might, and probably did, conceal a sniper, and every hill a band of fanatics whose entry to Paradise could be ensured by the killing of a Christian.

The war's official account records that frontier fighting requires, at its core:

...the infantry... to cultivate a dash, and a desire to close with the enemy with the bayonet. This should be combined with a high standard of individual weapon training and a stringent fire discipline. Keen observation and an intelligent use of the peculiarities of terrain are essential factors in the employment of

infantry in mountainous terrain.

Demonstrating these attributes to the full, the 2nd North Staffords were never found lacking. The battalion bore out that the brute force of infantry and the traditional factors of discipline, leadership and training were the decisive elements of the war.

Four thousand North Staffords' men lost their lives during the First World War and the Third Afghan War. Of these, sixty resulted from service in India, just shy of two per cent. Nonetheless, the scale of deaths aside, the 2nd North Staffords had fulfilled a vital role. As one of the few regular army units kept in India during the world war, the battalion was an essential part of the sub-continent's *'thin red line'* of defence.

During the 1914–18 period, the battalion played no small part in subduing the frontier tribesmen, who were keen to exploit Britain's focus on the Western Front and elsewhere. A reverse in one area of the frontier could have proved the catalyst for disturbance and rebellion throughout the frontier tribes. The threat of a frontier rebellion was rekindled by the Third Afghan War. Combined with calls for independence, the war had the potential to set-off an anti-British uprising across India. The North Staffords had a pivotal role in preventing this. First, by halting the planned uprising in Peshawar, which could have emboldened the tribesmen and swung their support for the Afghan invasion. Second, by resolutely ejecting the Afghans from Khargali Ridge after the first attack by a British brigade had stalled. Had the battalion failed in this task, the second brigade attack would likely have been lost. If it had been, the Afghans would have gained time to reinforce their positions and shift to the offensive. Given the rugged terrain of the Khyber and Afghan control of the water supply, further British attempts to repel the invasion may have been severely compromised. Finally, the battalion led the Anglo-Indian force into Afghanistan, clearing the path for the limited invasion that followed, and then maintaining the security of this vital route. Failure in the Khyber region was almost certain to have mobilised the frontier tribesmen to unite with the Afghan regulars. Fighting this joint force, across an extended front and for a prolonged period, likely aggravated by a widespread insurrection across India, would have been a severe test for the British.

Fortunately, aided by the North Staffords, history took a different course.

"SAVE ME FROM MY FRIENDS!"

Figure 1: Great Game cartoon, showing the Amir of Afghanistan with his 'friends' Russia and Great Britain, 1878.

Figure 2: Captain Eustace Jotham V.C. (posthumously awarded), a former North Staffords' officer.

Figure 3: Shabkadr Fort on the North-West Frontier, 1915.

Figure 4: 2nd North Staffords' soldiers resting outside Shabkadr Fort in autumn 1915. Note the humorous caption over-written onto the cow.

Figures 5 & 6: Major Henry Tweedie, Officer Commanding C Company (*left*) and Captain Alfred Punchard, Adjutant (*right*), 2nd North Staffords (during the North-West Frontier campaign, 1915).

Figure 7: No. 8 (Mountain) Battery, Royal Garrison Artillery shelling Hafiz Kor village on 8 October, 1915.

Figure 8: 2nd North Staffords' soldiers removing the wounded at Hafiz Kor on 8 October, 1915.

Figure 9: Officers and soldiers of the 2nd North Staffords crossing a barge bridge on the route from Shabkadr to Peshawar in October, 1915.

Figure 10: Amanullah Khan, Amir of Afghanistan, 1919-1929.

Figure 11: Lieutenant Colonel Edward Vigor Fox, 2nd North Staffords commanding officer, 1914-1920 *(unconfirmed image)*.

Figure 12: A bazaar scene in Peshawar City, 1919.

Figure 13: An Afghan regular army soldier, 1919.

Figure 14: A camel convoy at the entrance to the Khyber Pass, 1919.

Figure 15: A view of 2nd North Staffords' soldiers marching up the
Khyber Pass.

Figure 16: British airpower on the frontier, 1919.

Figure 17: In the Khyber Pass, looking north on the approach to Ali
Masjid Fort. The ambush of B Company on 9 May 1919 would have
been in the vicinity of this area.

Figure 18: Ali Masjid Fort (*top-left*) and the entrance to the defile (*centre-right*).

Figure 19: Landi Kotal Fort (*centre-left*) and camp area.

James Green

BRIGHTS HILL Sq.L.7. - STAFFORD RIDGE.

11th   0430   The Battalion strength 18 officers
      hrs   511 other ranks paraded at 0430
           hrs and marched to Rendezvous
           BRIGHTS HILL distance about 2 mls.
           objectives pointed out to O.C.
           Coys. from this place. At 07.48
           hrs all ready for attack which
           commenced at 0810 hrs ground very
           difficult and final ascent very
           steep the position was captured at   Na:
           1045 hrs. Order of advance B, D,   se:
           C, A. A Coy. covered the advance   Bd:
           from a position on left flank
           during the attack from the jumping
           off place i.e. 1200^X E.of point
           4596 Square L.8. the leading lines

Figure 20: Extract from the 2nd North Staffords' war diary for the
Khargali Ridge attack on 11 May 19.

Figure 21: A view of Khargali Ridge (*top-left to centre*), Bagh Springs
(*middle-centre, amongst the scrub and foliage*) and Kafir Kot Ridge (*top-right*). Scene of the Second Battle of Bagh, 11 May 1919.

Figure 22: Private Percy Wick D.C.M., 2nd North Staffords.

Figure 23: 2nd North Staffords troops, after their attack, on the Afghan position at Khargali Ridge on 11 May 1919.

Figure 24: Private Ernest Pepper, 2nd North Staffords. A bandsman, he was wounded at the Second Battle of Bagh but survived.

Figure 25: British soldiers escort an Afghan prisoner, 1919.

Figure 26: Field graves of Private John Ware and Private William Simpson, 2nd North Staffords, killed at the Second Battle of Bagh.

Figure 27: An Indian Army sentry overlooks Bagh village and the Tangi springs beyond.

Figure 28: Landi Khana camp in the lower Khyber, looking north-west towards Afghanistan.

Figure 29: A view of the border between British India with Afghanistan in the lower Khyber.

Figure 30: Entering the Dakka Plain, 1919.

Figure 31: In Afghan territory, the British camp in the Dakka Plain with the Kabul River in the middleground.

Figure 32: Beyond the British camp at Dakka looking towards Jalalabad. Taken from a piquet during an engagement. Note the troops next to the Jalalabad Road (*centre-left*) and the smoke or dust plumes further along the road, beyond the two hills in the middle-ground (*centre*).

Figure 33: An Afridi tribesman from the Khyber.

Figure 34: 2nd North Staffords' piquet at the Tangi *nullah*.

Figure 35: No. 7 piquet on the spur of Kafir Kot Ridge, looking north-west into Afghanistan.

Figure 36: 2nd North Staffords' troops at the Khargali South piquet, with a Lewis Gun in the foreground.

Figure 37: Lieutenant E. L. G. Beville, Officer Commanding A Company, 2nd North Staffords (*image taken during officer training*).

Figure 38: Arrival of the Afghan peace delegates at Dakka, 24 July 1919.

Figures 39 & 40: India General Service Medal 1908-1935, with
'Afghanistan N.W.F. 1919' clasp (obverse, *left*) and (reverse, *right*).

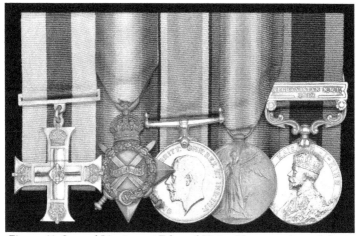

Figure 41: Second Lieutenant Edward Victor Horseman's medal set, showing (*left-right*), the Military Cross, 1914-1915 Star, British War Medal, Victory Medal and India General Service Medal 1908-1935, with 'Afghanistan N.W.F. 1919' clasp.

Figure 42: Private Percy Wick's Distinguished Conduct Medal (reverse).

Figure 43: 2nd North Staffords' men wearing their medals, 1923 (possibly including Sergeant Arthur Redfern, D.C.M., *middle row-sixth from left*).

Figure 44: Metal capbadge worn by men of The Prince of Wales's (North Staffordshire) Regiment.

Appendices

The Prince of Wales's (North Staffordshire) Regiment - a short history

'The Black Knots'

The origins of the Prince of Wales's (North Staffordshire) Regiment go back to 1756 when the 2nd Battalion of the 11th (Devonshire) Regiment of Foot was raised. Two years later the battalion became a regiment in its own right and was designated as the 64th Regiment of Foot. The 64th had a long history of overseas service starting, almost immediately, with a deployment to the West Indies during the Seven Years War. It also saw action in the American Revolutionary War taking part in the first and last clashes of the war. In 1782 the regiment was re-titled the 64th (2nd Staffordshire) Regiment of Foot, beginning its long association with the county of Staffordshire. In the 1790s it served in the West Indies, South America and Canada during the Napoleonic Wars. Then, in France, as part of the army of occupation after the Battle of Waterloo. After many years of peacetime service, the regiment fought in the Anglo-Persian War (1856) and served in British India during the Indian Mutiny (1857-58).

The other predecessor of the North Staffords was the 98th Regiment of Foot, later the 98th (Prince of Wales's) Regiment of Foot, which was raised in 1824. Like the 64th, it spent most of its time overseas. It served for thirteen years in South Africa before seeing action in China in the First Anglo-Chinese (or Opium) War and then transferring to India. As the East India Company pushed westwards, the 98th was one of the first British units to serve on the North-West Frontier (1849-51). It returned there in 1858 and remained in India until 1867. A seven-year tour of the West Indies followed in 1873. During the Cardwell Reforms of the 1870s, the 98th became linked to the 64th. From then on, the two regiments shared a recruiting district and single training depot, at Whittington, near Lichfield in Staffordshire. At the tail end of the Second Anglo-Afghan War in 1880, the 98th moved back to the Indian subcontinent where it was based in the port city of Karachi. It did not take part in operations within Afghanistan itself.

In the same month that the Second Afghan War concluded, May 1881, the British Secretary of State for War, Hugh Childers, issued General Order 41/1881. Known as the Childers Reforms, this order continued the Cardwell Reforms. It reorganised infantry regiments further, abolishing seniority numbers and merging single battalion regiments together. So, on 1 July 1881, the 64th and the 98th regiments of foot were amalgamated to form The Prince of Wales's (North Staffordshire) Regiment. These two regular regiments became, respectively, the 1st and 2nd Battalions of the new regiment. The Militia and Rifle Volunteers forces of North Staffordshire joined this new regiment. It recruited from the towns of the Staffordshire Potteries. Men of the regiment wore insignia which incorporated the Stafford Knot, the symbol of Staffordshire.

After the formation, the 1st North Staffords went, in 1884, to the West Indies. Deployments followed to Natal in 1887, Mauritius in 1890, Malta in 1893 and to British Egypt in 1895.

From there the battalion took part in operations in the Anglo-Egyptian conquest of Sudan. It played a key role in the action against the Dervish Army at Hafir, which was decisive in ending the campaign. The war earned the newly designated regiment its first battle honour, adding to the eleven already conferred on its antecedent regiments. After Sudan, the 1st Battalion served in India from 1897 until 1903. The 2nd North Staffords had remained in India after the Second Afghan War ended, later taking part in an expedition to the Zhob Valley in 1884. It returned to England in 1886, via Aden, and transferred to Ireland in 1893. In 1899, the 2nd Battalion deployed to South Africa, where it fought in the Second Boer War. The regiment's militia and volunteer battalions also took part and together the regiment earned its second battle honour. At the war's end in June 1902, the 2nd North Staffords returned to England and then transferred to India within a year.

It was in India that the 1st and 2nd Battalions met for the first time. To bolster the ranks of the newly arrived battalion for their service in India, the 1st North Staffords transferred the bulk of its men to the 2nd North Staffords. The reduced 1st Battalion then served for nine years in Lichfield and other stations in England, before moving to Ireland in 1912. In 1908, the Territorial and Reserve Forces Act 1907 reorganised the two militia battalions and two volunteer battalions which had joined the regiment on its formation in 1881. The militia were re-designated the 3rd and 4th Special Reserve, with the volunteer battalions becoming Territorial Forces and renumbered as the 5th and 6th Battalions.

At the outbreak of the First World War, the Prince of Wales's (North Staffordshire) Regiment had two regular battalions, two special reserve battalions, and two Territorial Force battalions. As the British Army grew to meet the demands of war, the territorials expanded. By the end of 1914 the regiment had six territorial battalions. These were organised into First Line (1/5th and 1/6th), Second Line (2/5th and 2nd/6th) and Third Line (3/5th and 3/6th). Added to these, following Lord Kitchener's famous call for volunteers in August 1914, were the 7th, 8th and 9th service battalions. Later the regiment raised 10th and 11th reserve battalions, followed by 12th and 13th service battalions and a 2nd (Home Service) Battalion. In total, eighteen North Staffords' battalions served in the First World War. Of those battalions which deployed overseas, the 1st North Staffords led the way. It served in France from September 1914 until November 1918. Nine of the other battalions deployed to either France or Belgium for part of the war. These included the First Line battalions, which joined those from the South Staffordshire Regiment to form the 137th (Staffordshire) Brigade of the 46th (North Midland) Division. The 46th was the first complete territorial division to arrive in France in March 1915. The battalions in France took part in many of the major battles of the war. Notable actions were the 1915 Battle of Neume Chapelle, 1915 Battle of Loos, 1916 Battle of the Somme, 1917 Third Battle of Ypres, and the Battle of Amiens in 1918.

Some of the new battalions served closer to home. These included the Second Line battalions of the North and South Staffordshire regiments which formed the 176th Brigade of the 59th Division. They rushed to Dublin in April 1916 to help quell the Easter Rising before shipping out to France in February 1917. Others operated as training battalions in the United Kingdom, or as garrison security units on the British mainland and in Guernsey. Less for the 2nd North Staffords, serving in India, the 7th (Service) Battalion was the only battalion to fight outside Europe. It took part in the Gallipoli Campaign from July 1915 until January 1916, when it evacuated to Egypt. It then remained in the Middle East, taking part in operations in Mesopotamia (now Iraq). From there it pushed into North Persia (now Iran) and the Caucasus where it fought against the Turks in Baku, Azerbaijan until the war ended.

By the end of 1918 the North Staffords' battalions had earned fifty-nine battle honours, adding to the thirteen the regiment and its antecedent regiments had earned before 1914. Amongst the military awards and decorations conferred on individuals were four Victoria Crosses. George V awarded these to Sergeant John Carmichael (9th Battalion), Lance Corporal William Coltman (1/6th Battalion), Acting Lieutenant Colonel Edward Henderson (7th Battalion) and, posthumously, to Lance Corporal John Thomas (2/5th Battalion). Lance Corporal Coltman, who had already earned a Distinguished Conduct Medal with bar and a Military Medal with bar, was the most highly decorated British soldier of the First World War.

In the early inter-war years, the 1st North Staffords served in the Irish War of Independence and in Gibraltar. Peace-keeping duties followed in the conflict between Greek and Turkish forces in Thrace in South East Europe. They transferred to India in 1923. After fighting in the Third Anglo-Afghan War in 1919, where it earned the regiment a further battle honour, the 2nd North Staffords moved to Egypt in 1920. It briefly returned to Lichfield, Staffordshire in 1921 before redeploying to duties in Ireland, alongside the 1st North Staffords. In the same year, the regimental title altered to be The North Staffordshire Regiment (The Prince of Wales's). After the Irish tour finished in 1922, the 2nd Battalion spent time in various home stations for the duration of the inter-war years. This period was broken up by two years in Gibraltar (1930-32) and a year in Palestine (1936-37). As for the North Staffords' territorial and volunteer battalions, these were all disbanded or placed into suspended animation at the end of the war, or shortly after it. In 1920, the 5th and 6th Battalions were reformed after the reconstitution of the Territorial Army. Later, in 1936, the 5th North Staffords converted to an anti-aircraft searchlight unit. It kept a loose affiliation with the regiment until 1940 when it transferred to the Royal Artillery. With the threat of war with Nazi Germany looming, the regiment raised a new 7th Battalion in 1939.

Therefore, in September 1939, the regiment comprised two regular battalions (1st Battalion and 2nd Battalion) and two affiliated territorial battalions (6th and 7th Battalion). At the outbreak of the Second World War, the 1st North Staffords was in India. Like the 2nd North Staffords during the First World War, it remained there for the duration of the war. They saw little action, apart from a limited role in the defence of the Andaman Islands during the Japanese invasion in 1942. A six-month deployment to Burma followed in 1943. Meanwhile, the 2nd North Staffords was one of the first units sent to France in September 1939, as the 1st Battalion had been in September 1914. They were in the British Expeditionary Force that fought in the battles for France and Belgium, before being evacuated from Dunkirk on 1 June 1940. The next three years were spent in England preparing for a German invasion. Once the threat of invasion had receded, the 2nd Battalion were sent to North Africa, where they campaigned in Tunisia. They were a lead unit in the Anzio landings on the Italian mainland in January and February 1944. The battalion continued to serve in Italy until January 1945, when it relocated to Palestine, where it remained until the end of hostilities.

Meanwhile, the 6th and 7th Battalions formed part of 176th Infantry Brigade, which included the 7th South Staffords. The brigade remained in the United Kingdom for most of the war as part of the 59th (Staffordshire) Infantry Division. In 1942, the army transferred the 7th Battalion out of the brigade and it served out the war in the Orkney and Shetland Islands. It disbanded in 1947. The 6th Battalion landed in Normandy in June 1944. It fought in the Battle of Caen, which lasted through to August 1944, at which point the 59th Division was broken up to provide reinforcements to other British units. Two further battalions raised during the war were designated as the 8th and 9th Battalions. These later transferred, respectively, to the Royal Artillery, and the Royal Armoured Corps, disbanding before the war ended. Between the regulars and the territorials, the North Staffords earned twenty-three battle honours between 1939 and 1945.

After the Second World War, in 1947, India secured independence from Great Britain. With no need to garrison that vast country, the British Army reduced most infantry regiments to a single regular battalion. Following these orders, the 1st North Staffords left India for the last time and moved, in 1948, to Egypt. There, they amalgamated with the 2nd North Staffords who had made a shorter move from Palestine. The new 1st Battalion remained in Egypt on garrison and security duties until 1950, when it returned to Staffordshire. A year later, the battalion transferred to the disputed port city of Trieste. In 1953, it deployed to Korea as part of the United Nations force maintained there after end of the Korean War. From Korea, the North Staffords were sent to garrison British Hong Kong.

In July 1957, a year after the 200th birthday of the North Staffords, a defence review ordered the merger of the North Staffordshire Regiment with the South Staffordshire Regiment. This was a sensible pairing which created a single infantry regiment for the county of Staffordshire. The origins of the South Staffords go back to 1705 when Colonel Luke Lillingston raised a regiment, later to become the 38th Regiment of Foot. It was raised in the King's Head Public House in Lichfield which can still be visited today. Under the

Childers Reforms, the South Staffords were formed from a merger of the 38th (1st Staffordshire) and the 80th (Staffordshire Volunteers) Regiments of Foot in 1881. The merger of the North and South Staffords took place on 31 January 1959 at Minden, Germany. Together the two regiments formed The Staffordshire Regiment (The Prince of Wales's).

The Staffordshire Regiment existed from 1959 to 2007. During that period, it spent time overseas in Kenya and Uganda and was the last unit of the British Army to serve in East Africa. It deployed to Sharjah in the Persian Gulf and was also the last unit to leave there when Sharjah joined the United Arab Emirates in 1971. Multiple tours of Northern Ireland and Germany followed. It was from the latter that the 1st Staffords deployed to Saudi Arabia and played a leading role in the 1991 Gulf War. Great Britain and Northern Ireland postings followed in the 1990s. And, there was a tour to Hong Kong in 1996, where it was the penultimate British infantry regiment to garrison the colony before its handover to China. In 2000, the Staffords joined the United Nations peace-keeping force in Cyprus and in 2002 it deployed to Kosovo. Its final deployments were to Iraq in 2005 and 2006-07. Many of these deployments were supported by reinforcements from 3rd Staffords, the regiment's Territorial Army battalion. This unit was disbanded in 1999 and replaced with The West Midlands Regiment, a single battalion territorial unit that comprised companies from four different infantry cap-badges.

In 2003, there was a further defence review. This one set the Staffordshire Regiment on course to merge with its neighbouring county regiments, the Cheshire Regiment, and the Worcestershire and Sherwood Foresters Regiment (29th/ 45th Foot). The new regiment, The Mercian Regiment (Cheshires, Worcesters and Foresters, and Staffords) was created in 2007. It comprised three regular battalions and one reserve battalion (the core of which came from the West Midlands Regiment, which disbanded in 2007). Each of the Mercian battalions deployed overseas, with the regiment conducting multiple tours of Afghanistan and Iraq. After the end of combat operations in the Gulf War (2003-11) and Afghanistan (2002-14), the Government ordered further reductions in the British infantry. Accordingly, in 2014, the Mercians reduced its number of regular battalions from three to two.

In its short history, the Mercian Regiment has earned a reputation as an outstanding fighting regiment. Today, it is one of the premier infantry regiments of the British Army and continues the traditions of the North Staffords and its other antecedent regiments.

*****

The history of the North Staffordshire Regiment is told in further detail at The Staffordshire Regiment Museum in Lichfield, Staffordshire.

The Khyber Pass

Described by Kipling as *'a sword cut through the mountains'*, the Khyber Pass is the most northerly and important of the mountain passes between Afghanistan and Pakistan, formerly British India. The Pass has historically been the gateway for invasions of the Indian subcontinent from the north-west. Through it have passed Persians, Greeks, Mughals and Afghans. It was the scene of battles between the Afghans and the British in all three of the Anglo-Afghan Wars. Aside from its military importance, the Pass is an important trading route, part of the Silk Road, which links southern and eastern Asia with the West.

Connecting Jalalabad in Afghanistan to Peshawar in India, the Pass cuts a thirty-three-mile path through the Spin Ghar (Safēd Kōh) Mountains. These are a series of broken hills that off-shoot from the larger Hindu Kush range. From its eastern entrance near Jamrud Fort (at an altitude of 475 metres), the Pass ascends steeply. A small fort, Fort Maude, is located six miles in. The gradient then levels off on the approach to Ali Masjid Fort (800 metres), eleven miles along the route. Here, the Pass opens into a valley dominated by a British fort. Beyond Ali Masjid the Pass becomes a defile of no more than 180 metres wide, for five miles, flanked by towering cliffs. Gradually the defile widens into small valleys scattered with villages and cultivation plots. About nine miles west of Ali Masjid is Landi Kotal Fort and cantonment, the highest point in the Pass (1,080 metres). In 1919, the fort was the main British garrison for the Khyber Rifles. There, the summit widens out northward for two miles. From Landi Kotal the main pass descends, passing the Bagh and Tangi Springs, to a smaller valley at Landi Khana (800 metres). It then runs through another gorge before entering Afghanistan territory at Torkham (730 metres). Not far beyond is the old Afghan fort of Haft Chah. Thereafter the route winds another ten miles down to the barren Dakka Plain (425 metres), alongside the Kabul River.

In 1919, transit routes through the Pass comprised a track for camel and mule caravans and a recently constructed gravelled road for wheeled vehicles. As the Third Afghan War was fought, the route was enhanced. Improvements included an aerial ropeway for moving supplies up from Jamrud; although this was not fully operational by the time the war ended. Later, in 1925, a railway was extended up to Landi Kotal.

The name Khyber can be applied to the wider province around the Pass, amongst which live various tribes. These include the Afridis and the Afghan Shinwaris, who both live within the Pass itself.

Timeline

A selective timeline of events during the Third Afghan War, 1919 is below. It focuses on events involving the 2nd North Staffords.

February 1919

20 February: Habibullah Khan, Amir of Afghanistan, assassinated and Amanullah Khan (Habibullah's son) assumes the throne.

March 1919

3 March: The new Amir writes to Viscount Chelmsford, Viceroy of India, requesting that Afghanistan be a free and independent nation. Viscount Chelmsford later denies the request.

May 1919

3 May: Amanullah Khan declares a *jihad* against Britain. Tribesmen block a detachment of Khyber Rifles near to the Landi Kotal border garrison and kill five unarmed road labourers.

4 May: Afghan regulars cross into British territory and cut off the water supply to the Landi Kotal garrison. The Afghan Postmaster in Peshawar distributes leaflets calling for Muslims in the city to revolt.

5 May: A small column of British reinforcements from the 1st Brigade is sent to Landi Kotal. More Afghan regulars cross into British territory and build up defensive positions near Bagh.

6 May: Viscount Chelmsford declares war on Afghanistan.

7 May: The remaining units of the 1st Brigade are moved up into the Khyber to relieve Landi Kotal. The 2nd Brigade, including the 2nd North Staffords, are mobilised and move up to Peshawar.

8 May: The 2nd North Staffords, 2/11th Gurkhas and 1st King's Dragoon Guards contain a planned insurrection in Peshawar City.

9 May: The 1st Brigade attack the Afghan positions at Bagh, but the attack fails. 2nd North Staffords' troops are ambushed by tribesmen as they march up into the Khyber Pass. Aircraft are used offensively for the first time in South Asia.

10 May: The 2nd North Staffords and the remaining elements of the 2nd Brigade arrive in Landi Kotal.

11 May: The 2nd Brigade attack the Afghan positions at Bagh, supported by 1st Brigade units. The 2nd North Staffords lead the assault on the Khargali Ridge. After a tough battle, the British defeat the Afghan regulars.

12 May: Afghan regulars advance across the border in the Chitral and seize Arnawai.

13 May: Elements of the 1st and 2nd brigades (including some North Staffords' personnel) cross the border, becoming the first British troops to enter Afghanistan since 1881. The 1st Cavalry Brigade push through the infantry to secure the Dakka Plain.

15 May: The 2nd North Staffords establish a camp at Landi Khana, providing piquets to protect the route to the Afghan border.

16 May: A British reconnaissance force near the Dakka Plain encounters a reserve force of 3,000 Afghan regulars. The recce troops are forced to retire, carrying out the last mounted charge of the British cavalry in the Indian sub-continent to break contact, whilst the Afghans pursue and attack the British camp at Dakka.

17 May: After a night advance and a dawn assault, the British at Dakka attack the Afghan lines. Almost stalling, the British attack succeeds, and the Afghans retire in disarray.

18 May: The British start preparations to advance to Jalalabad.

21 May: Intelligence received that General Nadir Khan was intending to advance into Waziristan.

23 May: Chitrali Militia succeed in driving the Afghans back across the border.

24 May: Afghan regular army troops, supported by tribesmen, cross into Waziristan. Militia posts abandoned and widespread desertions in North and South Waziristan. A lone Handley Page V/1500 bomber conducts an aerial bombing sortie on the Afghan capital, Kabul.

27 May: The British military post at Thal in Waziristan is attacked by Afghan regulars. Further south, in Balochistan, the British cross into Afghanistan to seize the Spin Boldak Fort.

28 May: Amanullah writes to the Viceroy of India requesting peace.

31 May: Brigadier Dyer arrives at Thal with a relief force.

June 1919

2 June: Successful British attacks in the Upper Kurram.

3 June: Viscount Chelmsford receives the request for peace, orders an immediate ceasefire and halts the planned advance on Jalalabad.

22 June: A 2nd North Staffords' piquet is ambushed.

28 June: Paris Peace Conference concludes, and the Treaty of Versailles is signed, formally ending the First World War.

July 1919

9 July: A 2nd North Staffords' piquet is ambushed.

26 July: Rawalpindi Peace Conference starts.

August 1919

8 August: Treaty of Rawalpindi signed. The Third Anglo-Afghan War officially ends.

September 1919

9 September: The 2nd North Staffords arrive back at their peacetime barracks in Nowshera.

1st Division - order of battle

The 1st Division was one of three divisions, three frontier brigades and four cavalry brigades maintained in the north of India for the purpose of defending the Indo-Afghan frontier, and which were mobilised to fight in the Third Afghan War. The headquarters and peacetime locations of the 1st Division's major units are provided below, together with the names of their formation commanders.

1st Division (Major General C. A. Fowler CB DSO), headquartered at Peshawar, alongside the headquarters of North-West Frontier Force, commanded by General Sir A. Barrett GCB GCSI KCVO ADC.

1st Infantry Brigade (Brigadier General G. F. Crocker CB)

Headquarters	Peshawar
2nd Battalion, The Somerset Light Infantry	Peshawar
1st Battalion, 15th Sikh Regiment	Peshawar
1st Battalion, 35th Sikh Regiment	Peshawar
1st Battalion, 9th Gurkha Rifles	Peshawar

2nd Infantry Brigade (Major General S. H. Climo CB DSO)

Headquarters	Nowshera
2nd Battalion, North Staffordshire Regiment	Nowshera
1st Battalion, 11th Gurkha Rifles	Nowshera
2nd Battalion, 11th Gurkha Rifles	Nowshera
2nd Battalion, 123rd Outram's Rifles	Nowshera

3rd Infantry Brigade (Major General A. Skeen CMG)

Headquarters	Abottabad
1st Battalion, The Yorkshire Regiment	Peshawar
2nd Battalion, 1st Gurkha Rifles	Nowshera
4th Battalion, 3rd Gurkha Rifles	Kakul
3rd Battalion, 11th Gurkha Rifles	Kakul

Also under command of HQ 1st Division were artillery, engineer, supply and transport, medical and veterinary units, along with a squadron of lancers, two Machine Gun Corps companies, a pioneer battalion and a signal company.

As the war progressed, some of the original order of battle and formation commanders changed. For example, Major General Climo was transferred from the 2nd Infantry Brigade to command the Waziristan Force on 27 May 1919.

2nd North Staffords - nominal roll of officers

The following officers were serving with the 2nd Battalion The Prince of Wales's (North Staffordshire) Regiment at the start of the Third Afghan War:

Commanding Officer
  Lieutenant Colonel E. V. Fox*

Second-in-Command
  Captain (Acting Major) S. A. Tuck*

Adjutant
  Captain E. A. Squirrell*

Quartermaster
  Captain T. E. Lowther*

Transport Officer
  Lieutenant B. E. Thompson

Bombing Officer
  Lieutenant T. J. Stroud

A Company
   Lieutenant E. L. G. Beville (Officer Commanding)
   Lieutenant N. B. Ford
   Second Lieutenant S. Harris

B Company
   Captain F. Hatton (Officer Commanding)*
   Second Lieutenant G. G. Goode
   Second Lieutenant H. J. Horncastle
   Second Lieutenant E. V. Horseman
   Second Lieutenant C. Vining

C Company
   Captain J. R. Whyte (Officer Commanding)
   Second Lieutenant A. Dagleish
   Second Lieutenant A. R. Frewin

D Company
   Captain C. R. P. Hearn (Officer Commanding)
   Second Lieutenant R. Lacey
   Second Lieutenant L. A. Scantlebury

Other North Staffords' officers known to have joined the battalion during the war were:

Captain E. J. Keeling
Second Lieutenant A. B. Savory

* Denotes officers who also served in the North-West Frontier Campaign, 1915.

2nd North Staffords - killed in action

The following soldiers from the 2nd Battalion The Prince of Wales's (North Staffordshire) Regiment died as a result of enemy action whilst serving on operations in the North-West Frontier, 1915 and the Third Afghan War, 1919.

The North-West Frontier, 1915

Private G. H. Johnson   5 September 1915
(Battle of Hafiz Kor, buried in Shabkadr Cemetery)
Private D. Toft   5 September 1915
(Battle of Hafiz Kor, buried in Shabkadr Cemetery)
Private H. Chadwick   9 October 1915
(Battle of Khwaja Banda, burial site unknown)

The Third Afghan War

Private A. Chapman   11 May 1919
(Second Battle of Bagh, buried in the field)
Private W. J. Ody   11 May 1919
(Second Battle of Bagh, buried in the field)
Private W. A. Simpson   11 May 1919
(Second Battle of Bagh, buried in the field)

Private J. H. Ware   11 May 1919
(Second Battle of Bagh, buried in the field)
Corporal G. Lunt   14 May 1919
(Second Battle of Bagh, buried in Peshawar)
Private A. Payne   22 June 1919
(piquet attack, buried at Landi Kotal)
Private J. Malpass   22 June 1919
(piquet attack, buried at Landi Kotal)
Private A. R. Matthews   22 June 1919
(piquet attack, buried at Landi Kotal)
Sergeant J. H. Ryan   22 June 1919
(piquet attack, buried at Landi Kotal)
Private C. V. Keeling   13 July 1919*
(buried at Nowshera)

* It is possible that Private Keeling died of an illness rather than enemy action, as his cause of death is not recorded in the 2nd North Staffords' war diary and he died some distance from the frontline.

In addition to the soldiers listed above, at least another forty-five North Staffords' men died in India between 1914 and 1918. Of these, most were in the final days of the First World War, in October and November 1918. As no enemy actions are known of during the period of the deaths, it is most likely that the soldiers died from natural causes, localised outbreaks of communicable diseases such as cholera, or the global influenza pandemic that swept through India in late 1918.

2nd North Staffords - honours and awards

Battle honours

The Prince of Wales's (North Staffordshire) Regiment was awarded the following battle honours for service in India during the First World War and the Third Afghan War:

'North-West Frontier, 1915'
'Afghanistan N.W.F. 1919'

Awards

Awards conferred on officers and men of The Prince of Wales's (North Staffordshire) Regiment for gallantry or meritorious service during the Third Afghan War:

Distinguished Service Order
    Lieutenant Colonel E. V. Fox

Military Cross
    Captain F. Hatton
    Second Lieutenant E. V. Horseman

Distinguished Conduct Medal
  Corporal A. Redfern
  Private P. Wick

Meritorious Service Medal
  Company Quartermaster Sergeant R. Barker
  Company Quartermaster Sergeant W. Evans*

Mentioned in Dispatches
  Captain E. A. Squirrell
  Company Sergeant-Major E. G. Fogg
  Sergeant B. H. Philpot
  Sergeant (temporary) W. G. Jones
  Corporal A. Redfern
  Corporal G. Lakin
  Private J. M. Bloor
  Private P. Wick

No honours or awards were granted to members of the battalion for the North-West Frontier, 1915 campaign.

* This award does not appear in *The London Gazette*.

Campaign medals

The India General Service Medal (1908-1935) with the 'Afghanistan N.W.F 1919' clasp was awarded to all officers and soldiers who fought in the Third Afghan War.

The medal was instituted on 1 January 1909 for campaign service on the Indian frontiers. The obverse has a crowned bust of George V, impressed with the words 'George V Kaisar -I-Hind' (which is the Hindi and Urdu vernacular for 'Emperor of India'). On the reverse is a picture of Jamrud Fort with mountains in the background, below which is a tied branch of oak and laurel with the word 'INDIA' above. The ribbon is green with a wide, dark blue stripe down the centre.

Individual officers and soldiers who had also served in the 1915 campaign qualified for the 1914–15 Star; complementing the British War Medal and the Victory Medal they would have earned for their wider service in India during the First World War.

Other

Brigadier E. A. Fagan (late South Staffords), commanding 60th Brigade, was awarded the Companion of the Most Exalted Order of the Star of India, an order of chivalry.

Colonel (temporary Brigadier) C. O. Tanner (late North Staffords), commanding 65th Brigade, was Mentioned in Dispatches.

Glossary

Afridi	An ethnic Pashtun tribe
Amir	Arabic root: Lord, commander-in-chief, or leader, referring to the leader of the Afghan monarchy (king)
cantonment	A permanent military garrison in British India
CO	Commanding Officer (normally of a battalion-sized group), a military appointment
DSO	Distinguished Service Order, a military award
escalade	A scaling ladder used for siege warfare
firman	A royal mandate or decree issued by a sovereign in an Islamic state
GCB	Knight Grand Cross of the Most Honourable Order of the Bath, a British order of chivalry
GOC	General Officer Commanding (normally of a divisional-size group), a military appointment
Gurkhas	Abbreviated form for the Gurkha Rifles, an infantry regiment of the Indian Army

jihad	A struggle or fight against the enemies of Islam; a religious war
Lancers	Abbreviated form for several cavalry regiments of the British Army containing the title 'Lancers', normally preceded by a numerical designation (eg the 21st Lancers)
lashkar	A Persian word for an army or group of fighters
Mahrattas	Abbreviated form for the 114th Mahrattas, an infantry regiment in the Indian Army
MC	Military Cross, a military award
Mohmands	An ethnic Pashtun tribe
mullah	A Muslim scholar, teacher, or religious leader
North Staffords	Abbreviated form for the Prince of Wales's (North Staffordshire) Regiment, an infantry regiment of the British Army
nullah	A Punjabi word translated as an '*arm of the sea*', referring to a stream or watercourse, a steep narrow valley
OBE	Office of the Most Excellent Order of the British Empire, a British order of chivalry
OC	Officer Commanding (normally of a company-size group), a military appointment
Outram's	Abbreviated form for the 123rd Outram's Rifles, an infantry regiment of the Indian Army

piquet	A soldier or small group of soldiers performing a particular duty, especially one sent out to watch for the enemy
Punjabs	Abbreviated form for the Punjab Regiment, an infantry regiment in the Indian Army
RAF	Abbreviation for the Royal Air Force
RAMC	Abbreviation for the Royal Army Medical Corps, part of the British Army.
RFA	Abbreviation for the Royal Field Artillery, an arm of the Royal Regiment of Artillery, part of the British Army
RGA	Abbreviation for the Royal Garrison Artillery, an arm of the Royal Regiment of Artillery, part of the British Army
RHA	Abbreviation for the Royal Horse Artillery, an arm of the Royal Regiment of Artillery, part of the British Army
sangar	A small, protected structure (fortification), used for observing or firing from
Shinwari	An ethnic Pashtun tribe
Sikhs	Abbreviated form for the Sikh Regiment, an infantry regiment of the Indian Army
Somersets	Abbreviated form for the Somerset Light Infantry, an infantry regiment of the British Army

Endnotes

Introduction

'**Code-named Operation Enduring Freedom**': The United Kingdom's military contribution to the war in Afghanistan was known as Operation Veritas, Operation Fingal and, latterly, Operation Herrick.

Chapter 1

'**German wartime activity towards**': In parallel with their diplomatic mission to Afghanistan, the Germans also dedicated resources to developing anti-British elements in India itself. It formed an Indian Committee within the German Foreign Office with the objective of stimulating a national uprising in India. The committee intrigued with the Indian independence movement and seditionists in the country and elsewhere, including the Hindu/Sikh-based Ghadar revolutionary movement in the USA and western Canada. It also circulated a letter from Kaiser Wilhelm II to the princes of India telling them that Germany would release them from British oppression. Playing on Turkey's entry into the war, German agents propagandised that Indian Muslims needed to rise-up against British rule to join the jihad. Habibullah only tacitly supported this activity but did concede to allowing the German-backed Indian revolutionaries to declare a Provincial Government of India in Kabul.

'natural robber tribes, living': McKenzie, 1915.

'resisted stoutly and displayed': The London Gazette, 1916.

'were defeated with heavy loss': The London Gazette, 1916.

'This fine Battalion came': Capper, 1923.

'showed a fine spirit and great': The London Gazette, 1916.

'were so successfully carried out': ibid.

'No fresh cases of cholera': The deceased soldiers were Private R. Clay, Private S. Nash and Private C. Snashall.

Chapter 2

'Some of the causes of the Afghan': The Times, 1919.

'With the end of the First World War': Wilkinson-Latham, 1977.

'Afghan regular units... were': Molesworth, 1962.

'The tribal offensive was the basis': Robson, 2004.

'They crossed into British-Indian territory': The border was undemarcated in the Khyber, as either the tribes had removed the boundary pillars or else it was not practical to install them in places due to the mountainous terrain. Indeed, the actual line of the border was disputed, with Afghans claiming it ran through Landi Khana, whilst the British viewed Torkham as the border.

'Later in the day, down in Peshawar': Some accounts of the war indicate that Ghulam Haidar was more complicit in the call for a revolt in Peshawar than merely the distributor of the *firman*. Indeed, there is evidence that he may written to the Amir notifying that he was arranging an uprising and requesting that Afghan forces came down from the Khyber to support the revolt in the city. In which case, the *firman* was an indication of the Amir's support for this action, rather than the Amir being the instigator of it.

'use every possible means to kill': The London Gazette, 1920.

'I have ordered overwhelming force': Robson, 2004.

'On 7 May, the brigade's British infantry': The 2nd Battalion The Somerset Light Infantry, were one of the eight regular British infantry battalions retained in India during the First World War. The regiment was amalgamated with other units several times during the latter half of the Twentieth Century. In 2007, it was amalgamated further into the present-day regiment The Rifles.

'**With the mobilisation of troops**': Later, in late May 1919, a third force was created. Designated the Waziristan Force it was formed from troops allocated to the Bannu and Derajat areas within the North-West Frontier area of operations.

'**Alongside the North Staffords were**': The 2/123rd Outram's Rifles, an Indian Army infantry regiment, was formed in 1903. It traced its origins back to 1820 and the British East India Company's Bombay Army. The regiment's predecessors fought in the First Anglo-Afghan War and the Second Anglo-Afghan War, amongst others.

'**The gravity of the situation will**': Holmes, 1920.

'**The City commanded by Fort Bala Hissar**': Holmes, 1920.

'**Reinforced by the 1st King's Dragoon Guards**': Formed in 1685, the 1st King's Dragoon Guards were the senior line cavalry regiment of the British Army. They were amalgamated in 1959 with The Queen's Bays (2nd Dragoon Guards) to form the present day 1st The Queen's Dragoon Guards.

'**After being relieved by the**': In 1966, The Royal Sussex Regiment was amalgamated with several other line infantry regiments to form The Queen's Regiment. Later, in 1992, The Queen's Regiment amalgamated with The Hampshire Regiment to become the present-day Princess of Wales's Royal Regiment (Queen's and Royal Hampshires).

Chapter 3

'**His infantry reserve was**': The remainder of the 2nd Brigade having been delayed for 24 hours to contain the situation in Peshawar.

'**To support them were**': No. 8 (Mountain) Battery had supported the 2nd North Staffords in combat before, during their attack on Hafiz Kor village in October 1915. Since that time, the battery had replaced their 10-pounder field guns with the 3.7-inch howitzer.

'**Fowler kept the 1/9th Gurkhas and 1/35th Sikhs**': The headquarters and one and a half battalions of the 3rd Brigade (4/3rd and 2/1st Gurkhas), reached Landi Kotal during the 11 May, relieving 1/9th Gurkhas to provide an additional reserve for the attack.

'In position at 7.48 a.m., the': There is a discrepancy in the time of H-Hour within various accounts. The Official Account, 1926 records it as 8.30 a.m. but the 2NSR War Diary, 1919 (*see Figure 20*) states H-Hour was at 8.10 a.m.

'ground very difficult and': 2NSR War Diary, 1919.

'The heat and the steepness': Official Account, 1926.

'He got himself up and pushed': After Second Lieutenant Horseman was wounded in the Second Battle of Bagh, he was evacuated to Peshawar and embarked for England in August 1919.

'Close behind, exploiting the breakthrough': Note that the official account states that it was the 2/123rd Outrams who captured the ridge, but other evidence suggests it was the 2/11th Gurkhas who occupied the ridge in the first instance.

'The Afghans had not fought badly': Robson, 2004.

'I thank all ranks, British and Indian': Capper, 1923.

'To: O.C. STAFFORDS.': 2NSR War Diary, 1919.

'dash and energy': Official Account, 1926.

'Later, Commander-in-Chief India': The London Gazette, 12 Mar 20.

'keenness of the rank and file': ibid.

'Whilst some of the battalions complied...': Official Account, 1926.

'British Enter Afghanistan. Strategic Point Seized': The Times, 1919.

Chapter 4

'somewhat uncoordinated and disorganised': Report of a reconnaissance made by a small force under Colonel Macmullen towards Basawal on 16 May 1919, Simla, 1919 (File No. 4608-F-Operations), cited in Robson, 2004.

'After a preliminary bombardment,': Official Account, 1926.

'... we shall by so doing threaten Kabul': Viceroy to Secretary of State, No.

698-S, 21 May 1919-FPPS, August 1919, Part II, No. 253 (CP/55g), cited in Robson, 2004.

'My guns will give you an immediate': Wilkinson-Latham, 1977.

'had been fortunate in his subordinates': Robson, 2004.

'Amanullah has lit a fire that will': Schofield, 1984.

'Captain Copland... sent forward two': Official Account, 1926.

Chapter 5

'The army... had coped admirably': Robson, 2004.

'resolutely opposed to going all': Robson, 2004.

'in spite of the armistice conditions': Robson, 2004.

'...a good example of troops at a': Official Account, 1926.

'At 1850 the piquet at KHARGALI S.': 2NSR War Diary, 1919.

'The Amir seems to forget it was': cited in Robson, 2004.

'28/29th July   0115 hrs': 2NSR War Diary, 1919.

'7th August': 2NSR War Diary, 1919.

'unquestionably won the peace': The Times, 1919.

'the speed with which the British': Robson, 2004.

'In return the Afghans agreed': This included the 'early demarcation by a British Commission of the un-demarcated portion of the [border] line west of the Khyber' (Treaty of Rawalpindi, 8 August 1919). Unsurprisingly, after the Delimitation Commission had finished its work, the newly built line of boundary pillars duly disappeared.

'I... [commend]... the fine military spirit': The London Gazette, 1920.

'Company Quartermaster Sergeants': The author has been unable to locate a London Gazette record for CQMS W Evans but his award has been mentioned in earlier regimental documents.

Chapter 6

'the most extensive and sudden': 2NSR War Diary, 1919.

'To the dead of the Indian Armies': CWGC, 2019.

'…viewed from the distance of time': Robson, 2004.

'a fine shooting battalion': Official Account, 1926.

'The two campaigns in which': Capper, 1923.

'…the infantry… to cultivate a dash': Official Account, 1926.

Bibliography

Books

Capper, J. E., 1923. *History of the 1st and 2nd Battalions The North Staffordshire Regiment 1914–23*, Longton.

Cook, H., 1970. *The North Staffordshire Regiment*, London.

Elson, J. C. J., 2003. *Honours & Awards: The Prince of Wales's (North Staffordshire) Regiment 1914–19*, Token Publishing, Honiton.

General Staff Branch, Army Headquarters India, 1926. *The Third Afghan War 1919: Official Account*, Naval & Military Press (repro ed, 2004), Uckfield, East Sussex.

Holmes, R. B., circa 1920. *The North-West Frontier of India in Pictures*, R. B. Holmes, Peshawar.

MacMunn, Lt Gen Sir G., 1935. *Turmoil and Tragedy in India – 1914 and after*, Jarrolds, London.

McKenzie, F. A., 1915. 'The Defence of India', *The Great War*, Vol. 4, Wilson, H. W. and Hammerton, J. A. (ed), The Amalgamated Press, London.

Miller, C., 1977. *Khyber: British India's North-West Frontier - The Story of an Imperial Migraine*, Macmillan, London.

Molesworth, G. N., 1962. *Afghanistan, 1919: An Account of Operations in the Third Afghan War*, Asia Publishing House, Bombay.

Robson, B., 2004. *Crisis on the Frontier: The Third Afghan War and the Campaign in Waziristan 1919–20*, Spellmount, Staplehurst.

Schofield, V., 1984. *Every Rock, Every Hill: Plain tale of the North-West Frontier and Afghanistan*, Salem House Publishers, Salem.

Wilkinson-Latham, R., 1977. *North-West Frontier 1837–1947*, Men-at-Arm series, Osprey Publishing (2005 ed), Hailsham.

Journals

The London Gazette, 1915. *Supplement to The London Gazette*, 23 July 1915, Issue Number 27545.

The London Gazette, 1916. *Supplement to The London Gazette*, 4 July 1916, Issue Number 29652.

The London Gazette, 1917. *Supplement to The London Gazette*, 30 October 1917, Issue Number 30360.

The London Gazette, 1918. *Supplement to The London Gazette*, 12 April 1918, Issue Number 30639.

The London Gazette, 1919. *Supplement to The London Gazette*, 14 March 1919, Issue Number 31235.

The London Gazette, 1920. *Supplement to The London Gazette*, 12 March 1920, Issue Number 31823.

The London Gazette, 1920. *Second Supplement to The London Gazette*, 30 July 1920, Issue Number 32001.

The London Gazette, 1920. *Third Supplement to The London Gazette*, 30 July 1920, Issue Number 32002.

The Edinburgh Gazette, 1920. *The Edinburgh Gazette*, 6 August 1920, Issue Number 13,621.

Other sources

The 2nd Battalion The Prince of Wales's (North Staffordshire) Regiment, 1919. *War Diary: 2nd Bn. The Prince of Wales's (North Staffordshire Regiment) 29th August 1915 to 9th December 1915 and 8th May 1919 to 9th September 1919.*

Websites

CWGC, 2019. *Delhi Memorial (India Gate).* [Online] Available at: https://
www.cwgc.org/find-a-cemetery/cemetery/142700/delhi-memorial
CWGC, 2019. *Karachi 1914–1918 War Memorial.* [Online] Available at: https://
www.cwgc.org/find-a-cemetery/cemetery/144300/karachi
DNW, 2019. *Orders, Decorations, Medals and Militaria (17 & 18 May 2016), Lot
80.* [Online] Available at:
https://www.dnw.co.uk/auction-archive/past-catalogues/lot.php?
auction_id=431&lot_id=275826
DNW, 2019. *Orders, Decorations, Medals and Militaria (17 & 18 May 2016), Lot
101.* [Online] Available at: https://www.dnw.co.uk/auction-archive/past-
catalogues/lot.php?auction_id=431&lot_id=275848

Credits

Images

Front cover, Figure 3, 4 , 5, 6, 7 , 8, 9, 11, 20: Originator unknown, reproduced by kind permission of The Staffordshire Regiment Museum Trust, Lichfield.

Figure 1: Tenniel, J. (1820-1914), image in the public domain.

Figure 2, 10, 24, 37, 43: Originator unknown, image in the public domain.

Figure 12, 17, 18, 19, 21, 29, 31, 32, 35: Holmes, R. B., reproduced by kind permission of The Staffordshire Regiment Museum Trust, Lichfield.

Figure 13, 16, 25, 30, 33: Originator unknown, courtesy of the Council of the National Army Museum, London.

Figure 14, 27, 28, 38, Back cover: Holmes, R. B., courtesy of the Council of the National Army Museum, London.

Figure 15, 23, 26, 34, 36: © Originator unknown, reproduced by kind permission Mike Simpkins.

Figure 22: Originator unknown, reproduced by kind permission of Dix Noonan Webb, London.

Figure 44: © Author.

Figure 39, 40: © Reproduced under licence from Hsq7278 / Wikimedia Commons / CC-BY-SA-4.0.

Figure 41, 42: © Dix Noonan Webb, reproduced by kind permission of Dix Noonan Webb, London.

Maps

Map 1: Shabkadr Area. Derived from Google Maps.

Map 2: Peshawar City. Derived from Official Account, 1926.

Map 3: The Khyber Pass. Derived from Google Maps.

Map 4: Second Battle of Bagh. Derived from Official Account, 1926.

Map 5: North-West Frontier. Derived from Gross, A., The Daily Telegraph Victory Atlas of the World, 1920 and MacMunn, G., 1935.

Map 6: Detail of Piquets. Derived from Official Account, 1926.

Index

Acknowledgements

With thanks to:

Danielle Crozier (curator), the staff and volunteers at The Staffordshire Regiment Museum Trust for their kind advice and support.

Michael Rutherford for his painstaking work designing the cover and drawing the maps.

About the author

Lieutenant Colonel James Green served in The Staffordshire Regiment, and then The Mercian Regiment, for twenty-five years. He was one of the first officers from the regiment to deploy to Afghanistan in 2003, following the 9/11 terrorist attacks two years before. Later, in 2005, he led NATO field intelligence operations for Northern Afghanistan. In this role he carried out an early reconnaissance of Helmand Province, ahead of the deployment of British Forces on Operation Herrick. He returned to Afghanistan in 2010 to lead a planning team responsible for building and training the new Afghan National Army. He has travelled extensively around Afghanistan and India. A graduate of the Royal Military Academy Sandhurst and the Defence Academy of the United Kingdom, he is a former trustee of The Staffordshire Regiment Museum Trust.

Back cover: Landi Khana camp in the lower Khyber, looking north-west towards Afghanistan.

Made in the USA
Middletown, DE
09 March 2025

72442900R00095